Giovanni

ISAT Coach
NEW EDITION

Coach™
America's Best for Student Success ™

Reading

LEVEL

D

Content Development by
The Mazer Corporation

Acknowledgments

Every effort has been made to locate the copyright holders for the selections in this book. The publisher welcomes information leading to the whereabouts of copyright holders for works in this book that do not appear in the acknowledgments below. Errors or omissions within the selections are unintentional, and the publisher is pleased to make corrections to future printings.

"The Cave That Talked: A Tale from the Panchatantra" retold by Jyoti Singh Visvanath, May 2004 issue of HIGHLIGHTS FOR CHILDREN. Copyright © 2004 by Highlights for Children, Inc., Columbus, Ohio. "The Cracked Chinese Jug" by Carolyn Han. Reprinted by permission of SPIDER, 2003, July, copyright © 2003 by Carolyn Han. "Down in the Valley" by Scott Erickson, February 1994 issue of HIGHLIGHTS FOR CHILDREN. Copyright © 1994 by Highlights for Children, Inc., Columbus, Ohio. THE EGYPT GAME. Reprinted with the permission of Atheneum Books for Young Readers, an imprint of Simon & Schuster Children's Publishing Division from THE EGYPT GAME by Zilpha Keatley Snyder. Copyright © 1967 by Zilpha Keatley Snyder. "Farming in Space" by Amy Hansen, November 2004 issue of HIGHLIGHTS FOR CHILDREN. Copyright © 2004 by Highlights for Children, Inc., Columbus, Ohio. "Fast Elephants" by Jack Meyers, Ph.D., June 2004 issue of HIGHLIGHTS FOR CHILDREN. Copyright © 2004 by Highlights for Children, Inc., Columbus, Ohio. "Footprints" by Beverly McLoughland, first appeared in SPIDER, August, 1999. Author controls all rights. "In the Drain" from STUART LITTLE by E. B. White. Text copyright © 1945 and 1973 by E. B. White. Used by permission of HarperCollins Publishers. "The Little Fly and the Great Moose" retold by Janeen R. Adil. Reprinted by permission of SPIDER, 1999, August, copyright © 1999 by Janeen R. Adil. THE LOST LAKE by Allen Say. Copyright © 1989 by Allen Say. Reprinted by permission of Houghton Mifflin Company. All rights reserved. "The Mystery of the Missing Spectacles" by Leone Castell Anderson, June 1996 issue of HIGHLIGHTS FOR CHILDREN. Copyright © 1996 by Highlights for Children, Inc., Columbus, Ohio. "Night Rides" by Beth Thompson, February 1993 issue of HIGHLIGHTS FOR CHILDREN. Copyright © 1993 by Highlights for Children, Inc., Columbus, Ohio. "The Old Men, the Young Men, and the Monkeys" by William Groeneweg. Reprinted by permission of SPIDER, 2000, June, copyright © 2000 by William Groeneweg "Orion" from THE SHINING STARS by Ghislaine Vautier and Kenneth McLeish. Copyright © 1981 by Kenneth McLeish. Reprinted by permission of Cambridge University Press. "Pay Attention, Donovan" by Barbara Youree. Reprinted by permission of SPIDER, 1999, July, copyright © 1999 by Barbara Youree. "The Real Princess" from ANDERSEN'S FAIRY TALES by Hans Christian Andersen, translation by E. V. Lucas and H. B. Paull. "Science Letters: Do Dolphins Sleep?" by Jack Meyers, Ph.D., January 2005 issue of HIGHLIGHTS FOR CHILDREN. Copyright © 2005 by Highlights for Children, Inc., Columbus, Ohio. "Things To Do If You Are the Rain" by Bobbi Katz. Copyright © 1982 by Bobbi Katz. Reprinted with permission of the author. "Sometimes on Monday Mornings" by Chuck Trapkus. Reprinted by permission of SPIDER, 1999, December, copyright © 1999 by Chuck Trapkus. "Taking His Best Shots" by Claudia Cangilla McAdam, April 2004 issue of HIGHLIGHTS FOR CHILDREN. Copyright © 2004 by Highlights for Children, Inc., Columbus, Ohio. Photo of John Fielder, courtesy of John Fielder. "Time to Change Clothes" by Marilyn Kratz, March 2004 issue of HIGHLIGHTS FOR CHILDREN. Copyright © 2004 by Highlights for Children, Inc., Columbus, Ohio. "Thumbprint" from IT DOESN'T ALWAYS HAVE TO RHYME by Eve Merriam. Copyright © 1964, 1992 by Eve Merriam. Used by permission of Marian Reiner. "What Do You Do When a Queen Comes to Visit?" by Mary Houlgate. Reprinted by permission of CRICKET, 2000, October, copyright © 2000 by Mary Houlgate.

We would like to extend a special note of gratitude to Andrew Jackson Language Academy for their help in developing this product.

ISAT Coach, Reading, Level D, New Edition
76IL
ISBN-10: 1-59823-001-8
ISBN-13: 978-1-59823-001-7

EVP, Publisher: Linda Sanford
VP of Production: Dina Goren
VP, Creative Director: Rosanne Guararra
Art Director: Farzana Razak

Development Editor: Amy Christensen
Content development: The Mazer Corporation
Designer: Farzana Razak
Layout artist: Joe Kaufman
Cover Design: Farzana Razak
Cover Photo: Bettman/CORBIS

Triumph Learning® 136 Madison Avenue, 7th Floor, New York, NY 10016
© 2006 Triumph Learning, LLC
A Haights Cross Communications, Inc. company

Table of Contents

To the Student

This book is called the *ISAT Coach, Reading, Level D*. It will help you prepare for the ISAT reading test.

Here is how this book will help you:

- It tells you what the reading questions on the ISAT test are like.
- It teaches you what you need to know to do well on the test.
- It has practice passages and questions like the ones you will see on the test.

The ISAT reading test has many multiple-choice questions. They are like the ones you will work with in this book. After each question, there are four possible answers. Only one is correct. The others are wrong. You must mark the one correct answer for each question.

The ISAT test also has extended-response questions. You will practice answering these types of questions in this book, too. Each time you see an extended-response question in this book, you will see an icon like the one on the right. This means you will have to write your answer on a separate sheet of paper as clearly as you can.

There are several sections in this book called Mix It Up: Cumulative Reviews. These reviews will test you on skills that you have already learned. They will also test you on skills that have not yet been covered in the book. Questions on the untaught skills are marked with a special box, like this ▮. Do not worry if you have trouble answering these questions. You will not be graded if you get them wrong. Just try your best!

Here are some tips that will help you when you work in this book and when you take the test:

- Read extended-response questions before you read the passage to see what your purpose for reading is.
- Read each passage carefully.
- Read each question carefully.
- Make certain that you answer the question that is asked.
- Use information from the text to support your answer.
- Ask yourself if the answer makes sense.
- Answer as many questions as you can.

Use these tips throughout the book and when you take the test. We wish you the best of luck on the ISAT!

NOTICE: Photocopying any part of this book is prohibited by law.

5

To the Parent

It is important that you learn as much as possible about the ISAT reading test. This book is called the *Coach*. It will help your child get ready for the ISAT reading test. Even though this book is for your child, you can learn a great deal about the ISAT test by looking at this book and helping your child with the lessons.

This *Coach* reading book is just like a good coach on a sports team. It explains step-by-step how to answer questions. It shows procedures carefully and clearly. It tells students how to get more points on the test. You can also help your child by checking homework assignments or quizzing your child on vocabulary words. There is a glossary at the back of this book you can use for this. Your child will feel more confident and less anxious about the test if you spend time reviewing at home.

Help your child work through the lessons. Encourage your child to read each question carefully, and to follow the steps in order. Make sure your child understands the answer to the question. When your child finishes the *Coach*, he or she will have mastered all the important ISAT Level D Standards/Benchmarks and Objectives that are on the test.

TEACHERS: Cut out this *Coach* **Parent Involvement Pledge** and send one copy home with each student to have signed by his or her Parent or Guardian.

Take the *Coach* Parent Involvement Pledge.

As a Parent, I pledge that I will:

1. Demonstrate to my child the value of education in everyday life
2. Help strengthen my child's reading skills by encouraging him or her to read something new everyday
3. Discuss with my child his or her class work on a regular basis
4. Keep communication open with teachers and principals and always participate in any parent-teacher meeting my child's school may host
5. Stay involved in homework projects

Because I know how important education is to success and to life, I pledge to be an actively involved parent in my child's education.

_____   _____
Parent Signature   **Student Signature**

Pretest

Session 1

> This is a flyer about joining a summer reading program. It was handed out to students in late May, just before summer vacation.

READY TO ENJOY YOUR SUMMER VACATION?
Join the Clark County Public Library's Summer Reading Program!
This year's theme is Reading Takes You Places.

Sign up between June 1 and June 15 to be a part of the fun. It is easy to get started.
Just fill in the form below and turn it in at any library branch.

When you do, you will receive:

- a log to keep a list of the books you read
- a fun rocket ship t-shirt
- a coupon for a free ice cream cone
- a button to wear with the program's theme
- passes to the bowling alley for two free games

Each week, bring in your reading log and we will happily stamp it so you can receive that week's prize.

Prizes include: free movie passes, a Frisbee disc, a silly ink pen, and other fun prizes.

When you have read the number of books you set as your goal, turn in your log at any branch.
   The deadline is August 15.
You will get a certificate, plus either a bookmark, a balloon, or a set of markers.

If you would like an extra reward, enter the Summer Reading Program Essay Contest. Write 250 words on the topic of "Where Reading Takes Me" by August 1. The top three essays will win a gift certificate for one paperback book from the **Young at Heart Bookstore**.

Fill out this form and take it to any library branch to get started!

YES, I want to be a part of the library's summer reading program.

Name: _____

Grade: _____   School: _____

Number of books I plan to read: _____

I plan to write an essay for the contest.

_____ Yes   _____ No

1. Which word has a suffix?

   Ⓐ Summer

   Ⓑ Program

   © <u>Happily</u>

   Ⓓ Branch

2. Which word has a prefix?

   Ⓐ Essays

   Ⓑ Internet

   © Certificate

   Ⓓ Watching

3. Which of the following is a compound word?

   Ⓐ Rocket

   Ⓑ Bowling

   © Bookstore

   Ⓓ Television

4. Which word means the same as <u>prize</u>?

   Ⓐ Contest

   Ⓑ Reward

   © Best

   Ⓓ Games

5. Which word means the opposite of <u>silly</u>?

   Ⓐ Tired

   Ⓑ Confused

   © Sad

   Ⓓ Serious

preview

incorrect

GO ON TO THE NEXT PAGE

TIME TO CHANGE CLOTHES
by Marilyn Kratz

> This is an article from *Highlights Magazine* that tells about birds molting, or changing their feathers, each season.

Isn't it fun to take off your sweaters and change into t-shirts every spring?

Some birds change their "clothes" in spring, too. They do it by molting. Molting means losing old feathers and getting new feathers to replace them. New feathers push the old, worn feathers out of the bird's skin.

Birds that live in harsh deserts and grasslands usually molt twice a year, in spring and in autumn. Their feathers wear out faster than those of other birds. Most other birds molt mainly in the fall.

Hiding from Enemies

Molting may take five to twelve weeks to complete. Ducks lose their feathers quickly. They are not able to fly until the new wing feathers grow in. They have dull feathers to help them hide.

Some birds become a different color when they molt. Ptarmigans have white feathers in winter, when snow covers the ground. In the summer they have brown feathers. Because their feathers change colors, ptarmigans can hide more easily all year long.

Looking for a Mate

Often male birds wear more colorful feathers after their spring molt. That is when they are trying to attract a mate. Egrets grow long, flowing plumes during spring courtship season. They shed the plumes soon after.

Getting New Colors

Some birds get a new color when the faded edges of their old feathers wear down. The inner part of the feather is a different color, and it begins to show. In spring, the male house sparrow gets his black "bib" in just that way.

Keep an eye on the birds you see around your yard. Maybe you'll catch them "changing their clothes."

6. What is the purpose of the bold print headings in this passage?

Ⓐ To define unknown words

Ⓑ To provide captions for pictures

Ⓒ To announce the next topic

Ⓓ To make the passage longer

7. How does the author explain what the word <u>molting</u> means?

Ⓐ She uses a synonym.

Ⓑ She uses a homonym.

Ⓒ She uses a definition.

Ⓓ She uses an antonym.

8. What inference can you make about egrets growing long plumes of feathers during mating season?

Ⓐ The females are attracted to those feathers.

Ⓑ The males need extra warmth during this season.

Ⓒ The long feathers give the males something to do.

Ⓓ The long feathers are all different colors.

9. What do you think was the author's purpose in writing this passage?

Ⓐ To convince you to look at birds

Ⓑ To teach you about molting

Ⓒ To entertain you with a story

Ⓓ To ask you to build a bird feeder

10. What generalization can you make about birds after reading this passage?

Ⓐ All birds molt twice a year.

Ⓑ Most birds grow long plumes of feathers.

Ⓒ Many birds lose their feathers and grow new ones.

Ⓓ Virtually all birds change colors when they molt.

GO ON TO THE NEXT PAGE

DOWN IN THE VALLEY
by Scott Erickson

> This is an article about California's Death Valley and all of the strange and wonderful creatures and plants that live in its arid climate.

It gave me a funny feeling to look up at a cliff and see a sign that says Sea Level. I was standing on dry land (very dry), but I was more than 200 feet below the level of the ocean, in one of the hottest and the driest places on earth.

You wouldn't expect to find much life in a spot like that. But what's amazing about California's Death Valley is that there's lots of life around.

The valley's many kinds of plants have to take advantage of every bit of rain (only about two inches of rain in an average year) to keep from drying up in the hot desert sun. Most plants grow on the bottom of hills and ravines, where a little water collects. The roots spread far and shallow to catch a lot of rain, or else they go down as deep as fifty feet to find water.

During the day it would be easy to think there are no animals here—except for some lizards scurrying around. Most animals hide in burrows during the day to avoid the heat, which often reaches 125 degrees Fahrenheit.

But at dusk the bats come out of their caves, swooping and diving through the air to catch flying insects. Coyotes yip and howl. And foxes, rats, and rabbits begin looking for an evening meal.

It's surprising how many plants and animals have found ways to make a living in a place as hot and dry as Death Valley.

write right

11. Which words from this passage are examples of onomatopoeia?

Ⓐ Hot/Dry

Ⓑ Hills/Ravines

Ⓒ Yip/Howl

Ⓓ Swooping/Diving

12. Which words from this passage are examples of <u>homonyms</u>?

Ⓐ See/Sea

Ⓑ Rain/Dry

Ⓒ Swooping/Diving

Ⓓ Plants/Animals

over

13. Which statement is the best summary of this passage?

Ⓐ The desert is a long way away.

Ⓑ There is a great deal of life in the desert.

Ⓒ Bats come out at night to eat insects.

Ⓓ It only rains two inches in the average year.

14. Which of the following statements from the passage contains an opinion?

Ⓐ But what's amazing about California's Death Valley is that there's _lots_ of life around.

Ⓑ Most animals hide in burrows during the day to avoid the heat, which often reaches 125 degrees Fahrenheit

Ⓒ And foxes, rats, and rabbits begin looking for an evening meal.

Ⓓ Most plants grow on the bottom of hills and ravines, where a little water collects.

15. What idea is implied about the author in this passage?

Ⓐ He thinks the desert is a wonderful place.

Ⓑ He has never spent any time in the desert.

Ⓒ He is eager to leave the desert.

Ⓓ He believes that little life is found in the desert.

GO ON TO THE NEXT PAGE

FINICKY FRED

by Tamra Orr and Annie Barnette

Read this poem about a fussy eater named Fred.

Finicky Fred loves to eat but he's picky!
Much more so than Sally, Peter or Vicky!

He only likes pickles and never tomatoes
He'll usually eat any kind of potatoes

He nibbles on crackers and loves things with noodles
He'll eat cherry pie, but rejects cherry strudels

He turns up his nose at corn and green peas
He runs away screaming at foods covered with cheese

He'll use kettles of ketchup and mountains of mustard
He loves sugary doughnuts but not if there's custard

He enjoys popcorn and pretzels and things that go "Crunch!"
He'll eat pizza for dinner, but never at lunch

He chomps on green apples and celery stalks
He pops his mouth full of grapes as he walks

Sometimes his mother says, "Try something new!"
If he does, he just swallows, and then he says "Ew!"

He frowns at clam chowder, he winces at beans,
He is the pickiest eater the world's ever seen.

But at least Finicky Fred is always polite
And remembers to say, "No, thank you" just right.

16. What type of literature is this passage?

Ⓐ Nonfiction

Ⓑ Myth

Ⓒ Story

Ⓓ Poem

17. Which phrase from the passage is an example of alliteration?

Ⓐ Chomps on green apples

Ⓑ Kettles of ketchup

Ⓒ Pickiest eater the world's ever seen

Ⓓ He loves sugary doughnuts

18. What kind of person is Fred?

Ⓐ Tall and thin

Ⓑ Polite

Ⓒ Physically active

Ⓓ An excellent student

19. Which of the following supports the main idea in this poem?

Ⓐ Fred always says, "No, thank you."

Ⓑ Fred likes potatoes.

Ⓒ Fred won't try clam chowder or beans.

Ⓓ Fred's parents do not mind if he is picky.

20. How does the writer support the idea that Fred is finicky about what he eats?

Ⓐ Through his words

Ⓑ Through his actions (what you do!)

Ⓒ Through his clothing

Ⓓ Through his location

Fred said, "I hate this food."

He'll eat pizza for lunch but at dinner.

GO ON TO THE NEXT PAGE

BREAKFAST OF CHAMPIONS

by Marianne O'Leary

This is a story about a special weekend family ritual—Dad's breakfast

---

Breakfast is the best meal of the day, especially on the weekends. During the week, there is only enough time each morning to eat cereal or maybe toast. But on Saturday and Sunday, my sister and I have enough time to play and watch cartoons as well as cook a breakfast feast.

Usually, my sister and I wake up late and then play or watch cartoons first. When our stomachs start to rumble, we head to the kitchen. Each Saturday and Sunday we take turns making our favorite breakfast foods. We love to make pancakes, waffles, French toast, and scrambled eggs. Our Dad usually joins us in the kitchen, and then the fun really begins. Dad loves to add what he calls "his secret ingredient" to whatever it is we are fixing. Sometimes he adds chocolate chips to pancakes. Sometimes he adds green pepper and cheese to our scrambled eggs. We have even seen him add a splash of vanilla to our French toast and waffles.

Most of the time Dad's secret ingredient makes our breakfast taste even more delicious.

Once, Dad decided to add a little of each leftover found in our refrigerator to our scrambled eggs. He called it "Everything But the Kitchen Sink." On that day, our scrambled eggs tasted as bad as they looked. Luckily, we had more eggs in the refrigerator and were able to start over. Dad didn't add a secret ingredient to that batch.

Last year Dad had to go to London for a business trip. He was gone for a whole month. We had to make breakfast by ourselves while he was away. We argued a lot while he was gone. First we argued about what to make. After grabbing the "Fabulous Breakfast Cookbook" from the shelf, we finally agreed to make waffles. Unfortunately, the arguing continued. We fought over who should crack the eggs and scoop the flour. Finally, someone (I won't say who, but it wasn't me) accidentally put salt instead of sugar in the waffle batter. Our waffles definitely weren't fabulous that morning. After that breakfast disaster, my sister and I ate everything but breakfast foods for breakfast. We ate frozen pizza, leftover spaghetti, and even peanut butter sandwiches.

We were so excited when Dad finally returned from his trip. Finally, we were able to have one of our breakfast feasts again! While we made our breakfast, Dad described some of the breakfast foods he ate while he was away. He said that in London they fry their bread for breakfast. Although Dad didn't enjoy the breakfast food on his trip he agreed that it was probably better than leftover spaghetti.

21. **What opinion does the author share about breakfast?**

Ⓐ Last year Dad had to go to London for a business trip.

Ⓑ Dad adds his secret ingredient to our breakfast foods.

Ⓒ Breakfast is the best meal of the day.

Ⓓ Every Saturday and Sunday we take turns making our favorite meal.

22. **What is the word root in <u>unfortunately</u>?**

Ⓐ Un-

Ⓑ Fortunate

Ⓒ -ly

Ⓓ Fortunately

23. **What is the meaning of <u>feast</u> in the passage?**

Ⓐ A highly enjoyed meal with lots of food

Ⓑ A snack

Ⓒ Food brought in from a restaurant

Ⓓ A meal made up of fancy foods

24. **What is the main idea of this passage?**

Ⓐ Making breakfast is hard work.

Ⓑ Dad's special breakfast is the family's favorite meal.

Ⓒ Fighting as you cook can ruin a meal.

Ⓓ There is not enough time to eat breakfast during the week.

25. **Which of the following events happened first in this passage?**

Ⓐ The girls ate leftover spaghetti.

Ⓑ The girls argued over who would crack the eggs.

Ⓒ The girls grabbed the "Fabulous Breakfast Cookbook"

Ⓓ The girls argued over what to make for breakfast.

GO ON TO THE NEXT PAGE

HOW TO MAKE THE WORLD'S BEST FRENCH TOAST

This recipe gives directions on how to make French toast.

What makes a good breakfast? In my family, a good breakfast always includes Grandmother's French toast. Grandmother learned this recipe from her mother, and has passed this recipe on to each of her children. Grandmother has recently started a new tradition. When each grandchild turns nine, she teaches him or her how to make this breakfast favorite.

What you need:

- 6 eggs
- 6 Tbsp. milk
- 1 tsp. cinnamon
- several drops vanilla
- 12 slices white bread, with crusts
- butter for cooking

In a large mixing bowl, stir the eggs, milk, cinnamon, and vanilla with three tablespoons of water. Carefully dip the bread slices into this mixture, one at a time. Make sure both sides are well coated. Lift the bread from the batter. Let any extra batter drip off.

While you are mixing the batter, melt a generous amount of butter in a heavy skillet. Lay a slice of bread in the skillet. Slowly brown the toast on both sides. Remove the bread from the skillet when both sides of the bread are lightly browned. Serve the hot French toast with maple syrup, butter, jams or jellies, honey, fruit slices, or corn syrup. This recipe will make enough French toast to serve six people.

26. **What opinion does the author share in this passage?**

    Ⓐ You should always melt a generous amount of butter in the skillet.

    Ⓑ Grandmother has recently started a new tradition.

    Ⓒ You should carefully dip the bread slices into the batter.

    Ⓓ Grandmother makes the world's best French toast.

    Opinion

27. **What must you do while mixing the batter?**

    Ⓐ Melt the butter in the skillet.

    Ⓑ Make sure that both sides of the bread are well coated.

    Ⓒ Serve the French toast with syrup.

    Ⓓ Let any extra batter drip off.

28. **How are the passages "Breakfast of Champions" and "How to Make the World's Best French Toast" different?**

    Ⓐ The passages focus on different meals.

    Ⓑ One passage is a poem and one passage is a story.

    Ⓒ The authors had different reasons to write the passages.

    Ⓓ The characters are the same, but the stories are told from different points of view.

    Opinion

    Fact

GO ON TO THE NEXT PAGE

29. What was the author's purpose in writing "How to Make the World's Best French Toast"?

Ⓐ To show how difficult it is to make French toast

Ⓑ To persuade people to start family traditions

Ⓒ To inform people about who makes the world's best French toast

Ⓓ To explain how to make the author's favorite breakfast food

30. Which step can be added to the beginning of the instructions?

Ⓐ Gather ingredients, mixing bowls, mixing spoons, and other materials.

Ⓑ Place the French toast on a plate.

Ⓒ Be careful not to drip syrup on your clothing.

Ⓓ Clean up your work space and wash the dirty dishes.

South Park is a television show.
South Park is the best t.v. show.

Session 2

NIGHT RIDES

by Beth Thomason

> Read this passage about a child's memory of car rides at night.

Sometimes we go for rides at night, when the sky is as soft and black as a cat. We might be coming home from Grammie's house, or going on a long vacation. And sometimes, we go riding in the evening just for fun.

We start our ride while it's still daylight. Then I watch the sun slide down behind the trees, and the sky lights up like fire. Soon the night turns as dark as a ripe purple plum. The stars twinkle on—one, two, three—as if someone had touched a switch. They are night eyes, watching us from so far away.

The cars turn on their lights, too, and my dad turns on ours. Soon, many pairs of round, white eyes are racing toward us, scattering the shadows. Ahead of us gleam small, red eyes, and we follow a friendly dragon along the winding road.

Night rides are full of lights. Traffic lights blink green, yellow, and red. Streetlights make white pools of light at each corner. Signs on stores spell out their names with tubes of glowing light, as if someone had written with a marker, right there on the night.

In the dark, we listen to the radio. It fills the car with music, and sometimes Mom and Dad and I sing along. And then I close my eyes and listen—to the song, to the engine's friendly purr and to the rushing sound of the night wind. The car rocks gently as we hurry through the dark.

When the engine stops, the quiet wakes me up. That's how I know I've been asleep. "Home again," whispers Mom.

Still humming the song, my dad carries me inside to my own bed. I hold on tight and hum the night song, too. And that's the best night ride of all.

1. **Why do you think that this person enjoys night rides so much?**

   Ⓐ They always go somewhere fun to play.

   Ⓑ He gets a snack when they go out.

   Ⓒ He likes being out at night with her family.

   Ⓓ He likes night time better than day time.

2. **Which sentence from this passage is an example of a simile?**

   Ⓐ When the engine stops, the quiet wakes me up.

   Ⓑ In the dark, we listen to the radio.

   Ⓒ The car rocks gently as we hurry through the dark.

   Ⓓ Sometimes we go for rides at night, when the sky is as soft and black as a cat.

3. **Which sentence from this passage is an example of a metaphor?**

   Ⓐ They are night eyes, watching us from so far away.

   Ⓑ Soon the night turns as dark as a ripe purple plum.

   Ⓒ That's how I know I've been asleep.

   Ⓓ I hold on tight and hum the night song, too.

4. **What type of literature is "Night Rides"?**

   Ⓐ Legend

   Ⓑ Folk tale

   Ⓒ Story

   Ⓓ Myth

5. **What inference can you make from this passage?**

    Ⓐ The main character does not like to ride in cars for very long.

    Ⓑ The family lives far out in the country.

    Ⓒ This is not the first night ride she has been on.

    Ⓓ The main character is twelve years old.

6. **Which of the following words is a compound word?**

    Ⓐ Watching

    Ⓑ Daylight

    Ⓒ. Vacation

    Ⓓ. Dragon

7. **Which of the following is an explicit idea?**

    Ⓐ There are a lot of lights to see during a night ride.

    Ⓑ The family only goes on night rides in the summer.

    Ⓒ The main character is a boy under the age of 10.

    Ⓓ These night rides last between 60 and 90 minutes.

8. **Which event in this passage is the climax?**

    Ⓐ Falling asleep to the sound of the motor and the wind.

    Ⓑ Getting in the car to leave for the night ride.

    Ⓒ Being tucked into bed when they get back home.

    Ⓓ Turning on the radio and singing along to it.

GO ON TO THE NEXT PAGE

9. **What is the author referring to when she writes about following a "friendly dragon"?**

    Ⓐ The sun setting in the sky.

    Ⓑ The large truck in front of them.

    Ⓒ The line of the cars' red lights.

    Ⓓ The song on the radio.

10. **What kind of characters are usually found in a myth?**

    Ⓐ Talking animals

    Ⓑ Military heroes

    Ⓒ Gods and goddesses

    Ⓓ Actual people

11. **Why is it helpful to read and compare two kinds of writing about the same subject?**

    Ⓐ You will spend more time reading.

    Ⓑ You will learn more about the topic.

    Ⓒ You will get a better grade in class.

    Ⓓ You will like one better than the other.

12. **What do you think the author's purpose was in writing this passage?**

    Ⓐ To entertain

    Ⓑ To inform

    Ⓒ To persuade

    Ⓓ To teach

13. **What word in this passage is an example of onomatopoeia?**

    Ⓐ Traffic

    Ⓑ Purr

    Ⓒ Dragon

    Ⓓ Lights

14. **Which phrase from the passage is an example of alliteration?**

    Ⓐ "sky lights up like fire"

    Ⓑ "signs on stores spell"

    Ⓒ "rushing sound of the night wind"

    Ⓓ "along the winding road"

15. **Which word contains a suffix?**

    Ⓐ Friendly

    Ⓑ Purple

    Ⓒ Radio

    Ⓓ Quiet

16. **What type of figurative language is found in the sentence, "Then I watch the sun slide down behind the trees, and the sky lights up like fire"?**

    Ⓐ Metaphor

    Ⓑ Simile

    Ⓒ Alliteration

    Ⓓ Consonance

17. **When do the night riders begin their night rides?**

    Ⓐ When it is still daylight

    Ⓑ After the sun goes down

    Ⓒ On the way home from work

    Ⓓ After breakfast

18. **What is the meaning of the homograph <u>wind</u> in the sentence, "We follow a friendly dragon along the winding road."**

    Ⓐ A blowing breeze

    Ⓑ To turn a knob to start a toy

    Ⓒ Blowing air

    Ⓓ To twist and turn

19. **What is the meaning of the homophone <u>right</u> in the phrase, "right there on the night"?**

    Ⓐ Correct or true

    Ⓑ On this point or place

    Ⓒ Appropriate

    Ⓓ A direction

20. **What happened after the night riders returned home?**

    A They turned the radio on and sang

    B They parked the car in the garage

    C The father carried the child inside

    D They went in to visit Grammie

GO ON TO THE NEXT PAGE ➡

21. What is an antonym of <u>whisper</u>?

Ⓐ Shout

Ⓑ Murmur

Ⓒ Mumble

Ⓓ Sing

22. What is a synonym of <u>hurry</u>?

Ⓐ Delay

Ⓑ Stop

Ⓒ Rush

Ⓓ Go

23. Which of the following actions does the child in the story enjoy most?

Ⓐ Visiting Grammie

Ⓑ Being with his mom and dad

Ⓒ Following the lights of the cars

Ⓓ Singing along with the radio

24. What does the word <u>gleam</u> mean in the phrase, "Ahead of us gleam small, red eyes"?

Ⓐ Glow

Ⓑ Watch

Ⓒ Wink

Ⓓ Flash

25. What type of figurative language is used in the sentence, "Soon the night turns as dark as a ripe purple plum."

Ⓐ Onomatopoeia

Ⓑ Metaphor

Ⓒ Synonym

Ⓓ Simile

26. Read these sentences. "Dad's singing had us in stitches. Even after he stopped singing, we could not stop laughing." What type of figurative language is used in the first sentence?

Ⓐ Simile

Ⓑ Metaphor

Ⓒ Omomatopoeia

Ⓓ Idiom

27. **What action shows that the child is very young when the story takes place?**

Ⓐ He sings along to the radio.

Ⓑ He rides in a car with his parents.

Ⓒ His father carries him inside.

Ⓓ He visits his grandmother.

28. **Which of the following words from the passage is a compound word?**

Ⓐ Someone

Ⓑ Racing

Ⓒ Humming

Ⓓ Parents

29. **Which of the following words from the passage contains a suffix?**

Ⓐ Parents

Ⓑ Purple

Ⓒ Bashful

Ⓓ Sometimes

30. **Which phrase from the passage is an example of consonance?**

Ⓐ "Ripe as purple plums"

Ⓑ "Sky lights up like fire"

Ⓒ "Scattering the shadows"

Ⓓ "Rushing sound of the night wind"

31. **How would the sights and sounds of the ride change if the ride took place on a bus? Use information from the passage and your own ideas to support your answer.**

GO ON TO THE NEXT PAGE ➡️

Pretest

Session 3

A HULA FROM HAWAII

This is a story about how one student and her mom came up with a unique idea for a school project.

Linda Simpson stared out of the kitchen window. It was a beautiful day. The sun was shining and only a few white clouds drifted across the blue sky. Linda never saw any of it though. She was too busy worrying.

"Isn't it lovely today?" asked Mrs. Simpson. "Linda? Hello, Mother to Linda. Are you in there?"

With a start, Linda turned around and saw her mother. One look at her daughter's face and Mrs. Simpson knew something was wrong.

"Are you still worrying about your school project?" she asked.

Linda nodded. "I have to tell my teacher tomorrow what kind of demonstration I am going to give about Hawaii. I still don't have any ideas about the kind of project I want to do. It seems like all of the other kids have really cool or really exciting ideas. Alex and Brendan are making a volcano that actually erupts. Alanna is bringing in food that she is making from her grandmother's favorite Hawaiian recipes. What can I do that would be just as much fun? I'm doomed!"

Just then, her younger brother Kevin came through the door. "Mom," he shouted, "Mr. and Mrs. Connors are back from their vacation. Come see what they brought us."

Mrs. Simpson patted her daughter on the arm and then went into the front yard to welcome her neighbors back home. They had just returned from two weeks in Hawaii!

"Hey," thought Mrs. Connors, as an idea came out of the blue. "Maybe they can help Linda."

A few minutes later, Linda found herself in the Connorses' living room. Her mother had found the perfect solution. Mrs. Connors had learned how to hula dance while she was in Hawaii, and she was going to teach Linda.

Mrs. Connors gave Linda a grass skirt to wear. She turned on some Hawaiian music and began moving her hips and her hands. Mrs. Connors asked Linda to come stand next to her. She showed Linda how to move her hands like slow rolling waves in the ocean.

"I always thought that hula dancers told a story with their hands," said Mrs. Connors. "But only part of the message is told with hand movement. The rest is told with words as you dance."

Linda grinned. This was going to be a fun lesson. It was going to be even more fun to show it off in school!

1. **Which event happens first in the passage?**

   Ⓐ Linda's neighbors come home from Hawaii.

   Ⓑ Linda looks out the kitchen window.

   Ⓒ Kevin comes into the house with an announcement.

   Ⓓ Mrs. Simpson goes outside to talk with the Connors.

2. **What is the plot of this passage?**

   Ⓐ Linda needs something for one of her classes.

   Ⓑ The Connorses went to Hawaii for vacation.

   Ⓒ Mrs. Simpson thinks it is a lovely day outside.

   Ⓓ Kevin is late getting home from school.

3. **Which of the following elements is part of the setting?**

   Ⓐ Character

   Ⓑ Plot

   Ⓒ Time

   Ⓓ Summary

4. **Who is the main character in this passage?**

   Ⓐ Kevin

   Ⓑ Mrs. Connors

   Ⓒ Mrs. Simpson

   Ⓓ Linda

5. **Which event in this passage shows the rising action?**

   Ⓐ Mrs. Simpson enters the kitchen.

   Ⓑ Linda learns how to hula dance.

   Ⓒ Kevin comes into the room with an announcement.

   Ⓓ Linda knows what to demonstrate in class.

6. **What phrase from this passage is an idiom?**

Ⓐ "The rest is told with words as you dance."

Ⓑ "Hey," thought Mrs. Simpson, as an idea came out of the blue.

Ⓒ Linda never saw any of it though.

Ⓓ A few minutes later, Linda found herself in the Connorses' living room.

7. **What was Mrs. Simpson's motivation to talk to the Connorses?**

Ⓐ To learn how to hula dance.

Ⓑ To see if Kevin was telling the truth.

Ⓒ To find out if they could help Linda with her project.

Ⓓ To ask if she could go on their next trip to Hawaii.

8. **What type of literature is this passage?**

Ⓐ Folk Tale

Ⓑ Poem

Ⓒ Myth

Ⓓ Story

9. **What is the suffix in the word demonstration?**

Ⓐ Dem-

Ⓑ -strate

Ⓒ Demonstrate

Ⓓ -tion

10. **What word from the passage above means the same as yelled?**

Ⓐ Turned

Ⓑ Patted

Ⓒ Grinned

Ⓓ Shouted

GO ON TO THE NEXT PAGE ➡

11. **What prior knowledge do you need to understand this passage?**

    Ⓐ Where the Connors and the Simpsons live

    Ⓑ What "Hawaii" is

    Ⓒ How old Kevin is

    Ⓓ The name of Linda's teacher

12. **What idea is implied in this passage?**

    Ⓐ Linda is a good dancer.

    Ⓑ Mrs. Connors has several children.

    Ⓒ Linda will learn to hula dance quickly.

    Ⓓ Mrs. Simpson doesn't like Linda's teacher.

13. **What event shows the solution to the problem in the story?**

    Ⓐ The Connors went to Hawaii.

    Ⓑ Kevin comes home.

    Ⓒ Linda is looking out the window.

    Ⓓ Mrs. Connors teaches Linda to hula dance.

14. **What word is an antonym of <u>grinned</u>?**

    Ⓐ Frowned

    Ⓑ Smiled

    Ⓒ Chuckled

    Ⓓ Listened

15. **What word best describes Linda's mother?**

    Ⓐ Uncaring

    Ⓑ Strict

    Ⓒ Helpful

    Ⓓ Angry

16. **"She showed Linda how to move her hands like slow rolling waves in the ocean." This sentence is an example of which type of figurative language?**

    Ⓐ Simile

    Ⓑ Metaphor

    Ⓒ Idiom

    Ⓓ Alliteration

17. Why was this passage written?

Ⓐ To persuade people to visit Hawaii.

Ⓑ To explain how to do the hula.

Ⓒ To share how one student overcame a problem.

Ⓓ To explain how to choose a topic for a school project.

18. Which shows the correct order of events?

Ⓐ The Connors return home, Linda complains, Mrs. Simpson has an idea

Ⓑ Linda complains, the Connors return home, Linda learns to hula

Ⓒ Kevin says the Connors are home, Linda learns the hula, Mrs. Simpson goes outside

Ⓓ Mrs. Simpson talks to Mrs. Connors, Kevin shares that the Simpsons are home, Linda learns to hula

19. Which of the following is a compound word?

Ⓐ Grandmother

Ⓑ Hula

Ⓒ Beautiful

Ⓓ Prepares

20. What might be another title for this passage?

Ⓐ Mom to the Rescue

Ⓑ Annoying Younger Brothers

Ⓒ Problem Neighbors

Ⓓ Linda's Lost Homework

GO ON TO THE NEXT PAGE ➡

21. **What does this sentence show about Linda? "It seems like all of the other kids have really cool or really exciting ideas."**

    Ⓐ Linda is bored by the ideas of her friends.

    Ⓑ Linda thinks her friends' ideas are silly.

    Ⓒ Linda is jealous of her friends' ideas.

    Ⓓ Linda is angry that her friends took her ideas.

22. **"Keep your chin up." This sentence is an example of which type of figurative language?**

    Ⓐ Simile

    Ⓑ Metaphor

    Ⓒ Onomatopoeia

    Ⓓ Idiom

23. **Which is a synonym of <u>doomed</u>?**

    Ⓐ Ruined

    Ⓑ Lucky

    Ⓒ Sad

    Ⓓ Nervous

24. **What do you predict might happen next in the story?**

    Ⓐ Linda makes a grass skirt.

    Ⓑ Kevin teases his sister.

    Ⓒ Linda is grounded for not finishing her homework.

    Ⓓ Linda shows her classmates how to hula.

25. **How did Mrs. Simpson know that something was bothering Linda?**

    Ⓐ Linda asked her Mom if she could talk.

    Ⓑ Kevin told his mom that Linda was upset.

    Ⓒ Mrs. Connors saw Linda crying and told her mom.

    Ⓓ Mrs. Simpson saw a worried look on Linda's face.

26. **Which meaning of <u>cool</u> is used in paragraph 5?**

    Ⓐ Unfriendly

    Ⓑ Somewhat cold

    Ⓒ Very good

    Ⓓ Acceptable

27. **"It's time for me to face the music." This sentence is an example of which type of figurative language?**

    Ⓐ Idiom

    Ⓑ Metaphor

    Ⓒ Simile

    Ⓓ Onomatopoeia

28. **Which of the following is a compound word?**

    Ⓐ Demonstration

    Ⓑ Something

    Ⓒ Volcano

    Ⓓ Tomorrow

29. **Which is a synonym of <u>beautiful</u>?**

    Ⓐ Lovely

    Ⓑ Unpleasant

    Ⓒ Nice

    Ⓓ Ordinary

30. **What is the main idea of the passage?**

    Ⓐ Sometimes help can come from unexpected places.

    Ⓑ You shouldn't wait until the last minute to do your homework.

    Ⓒ Hawaii is a good place to visit.

    Ⓓ Don't trust your friends.

31. **How do hula dancers tell a story without using words? Use information from the passage and your own ideas to support your answer.**

STOP

Unit 1
Vocabulary Development

Have you ever come across a word you didn't know when you were reading? It happens to everyone. It is important not to pass over an unknown word. Ignoring the unfamiliar word may make what you are reading seem confusing. Instead, stop for a moment. See if you can figure out its meaning. You may even have to go back and reread the passage.

In this unit, you will learn skills that will help you figure out the meaning of unknown words. You will also learn how to take a word and break it into parts. These parts are called **prefixes**, **suffixes** and **word roots**. You will learn what each part means, so that when you put them back together, they will make more sense.

In this unit, you will also look at the clues that surround new words. Sometimes these clues are found in nearby words and sentences. These clues can help you figure out new words' meanings.

Last, we will take a look at **synonyms**, **antonyms**, and **homonyms**. Knowing these words will help you to define words you have not seen before.

The more you understand about words, how they are put together, and how they can be similar and different, the better a reader you will be.

Try This

Work with a partner. Each student will need a piece of paper, index cards, and a pencil.

- Work together to brainstorm a list of prefixes (a letter or group of letters that is added to the beginning of a root word) and suffixes (a letter or group of letters added to the end of root words).
- Write each prefix and suffix on an index card.
- Brainstorm a list of simple base words. Write each base word on an index card.
- Take turns putting together cards with base words, prefixes, suffixes, or both. How many words can you create?
- Discuss how adding prefixes or suffixes to the word can totally change its meaning.

Lesson 1

Prefixes

A **prefix** is a letter or group of letters that is added to the beginning of a word root. It changes the meaning of the word in big—or small—ways. Here are some of the most common prefixes. Look at how just a few letters can change what the word root means.

Prefix	Word Root	Example
de–	part	*depart*
bi–	cycle	*bicycle*
non–	sense	*nonsense*
un–	easy	*uneasy*
re–	turn	*return*
dis–	agree	*disagree*
en–	courage	*encourage*
super–	star	*superstar*
sub–	way	*subway*

If you know what different prefixes mean, you can start to understand new words. Look at the following chart. How do prefixes change the meaning of a word root?

Prefix	Meaning	Example
bi-	two	*bicycle*
ex-	former	*ex-president*
in-, im-, il-, ir-	not	*impossible*
mid-	middle	*midnight*
non-	not	*nonliving*
over-	over, extra	*overworked*
pre-	before	*prefix*
re-	again	*remind*
sub-	under	*submarine*
un-	not	*unfriendly*
under-	under, beneath	*underneath*

How can prefixes change the meaning of words? Sometimes, adding a prefix can change a word to one that means its opposite. For example, if you add the prefix *un-* to *caring*, you get the word *uncaring*. In this example, *caring* means "to feel concern or to show kindness to another." The prefix *un-* changes the word to one that is opposite in meaning. The word *uncaring* means "not concerned" or "not interested."

Review the chart. Then answer this question.

Example 1

What does the word *unhurt* mean?

Ⓐ To hurt badly

● Not hurt

Ⓒ To hurt again

Ⓓ Hurting

This question tests whether you know what the prefix *un-* means. If you recall the chart, you know that it means "not."

Example 2

What does the word *discomfort* mean?

Ⓐ   Uneasiness, or not at ease

Ⓑ   For a show

Ⓒ   In favor of pain

●   Show something again

If you know that the prefix *dis-* means "not," then you can easily answer the question. You do not need to know at first what *comfort* means.

Sometimes more than one type of prefix can be added to a word to change its meaning.

re + appear = reappear

dis + appear = disappear

In this example, adding the prefix *re-* changes the meaning of the word to "appear again." The meaning of *appear* changes again when the prefix *dis-* is added. The new word that is formed means " to go away" or "to become hidden."

How does the meaning of *courage* change when you add the prefix *en-*? How does the meaning change when the prefix *dis-* is added?

en + courage = encourage

dis + courage = discourage

How can learning about prefixes help you be more successful in science, health, or social studies classes?

Try These

Replace the underlined words with a word that has the same meaning and contains the correct prefix.

1. He is <u>not kind</u>.

   Ⓐ Prekind

   ● Unkind

   Ⓒ Forekind

   Ⓓ Superkind

To help you figure this out, look at each prefix used. Which one has the same meaning as the word *not*?

2. Lucy <u>did not like</u> her new neighbor.

   ● Disliked

   Ⓑ Underliked

   Ⓒ Overliked

   Ⓓ Reliked

Narrow your choices by crossing out the words that use prefixes incorrectly.

3. Susan said to meet her in the <u>middle of the day</u>.

   Ⓐ Reday

   Ⓑ Unday

   ● Midday

   Ⓓ Foreday

4. The lights were quite bright <u>above her head</u>.

   ● Overhead

   Ⓑ Underhead

   Ⓒ Prehead

   Ⓓ Midhead

Lesson

2 Suffixes

A **suffix** is a letter or group of letters added to the end of word roots. Like prefixes, these groups of letters can also change the meaning of words.

Suffix	Root	New Word
-able, -ible	comfort	comfortable
-ed	watch	watched
-er; -est	tall	taller; tallest
-ly	quick	quickly
-ful	delight	delightful
-ing	interest	interesting
-tion	attract	attraction
-less	fear	fearless
-ment	enjoy	enjoyment
-ness	great	greatness
-ous; -eous	joy	joyous

Knowing what different suffixes mean can help you figure out unfamiliar words. Here are some of the most common suffixes and what they usually mean:

Suffix	Meaning	Example
-able; -ible	can be done	possible
-al	relating to	natural
-ance	state or quality of	annoyance
-er; -or	one who	teacher; actor
-ful	full of	beautiful
-ish	relating to	childish
-tion	act, process	graduation
-less	without	priceless
-ness	state or condition of	kindness
-ic	relating to	historic

Different suffixes can be added to the same word to create several new words. Each new word has its own new meaning. Add the suffixes *-ed*, *-s*, *-some*, *-er*, and *-ous* to the word *adventure*. How does each suffix change the meaning of the word?

Word	+ Suffix	= New Word	= New Meaning
adventure	-ed	adventured	*verb*, to have taken a risk
adventure	-s	adventures	*noun*, a series of exciting experiences
adventure	-some	adventuresome	*adjective*, inclined or likely to take risks
adventure	-er	adventurer	*noun*, one who takes risks or one who has exciting experiences
adventure	-ous	adventurous	*adjective*, likely to seek or contain unknown risks and dangers

Suffixes can also change a word's part of speech. For example, one of the most common suffixes is *-ly*. This suffix means "in the manner of," and changes an adjective like *quick* into an adverb like *quickly*. Look again at the chart above. Which suffixes changed *adventure* from a noun to a different part of speech?

Sometimes, a suffix can change a word to name a person's job.

write + -er = writer

journal + -ist = journalist

mathematics + -ian = mathematician

DISCUSS What words can you make by adding the suffix *-ly*?

Try These

1. **How does the word <u>perform</u> change if you add the suffix -<u>er</u>?**

   ● It changes from a verb to a noun.

   Ⓑ It changes from a verb to an adjective.

   Ⓒ It changes from a verb to an adverb.

   Ⓓ It changes from a verb to a pronoun.

   A performer is a person. Which part of speech identifies a person, place, or thing?

2. **Which word means "one who directs?"**

   Ⓐ Directness

   Ⓑ Directionless

   ● Director

   Ⓓ Directing

   Which word contains a suffix meaning "one who?"

3. **What is the suffix in the word <u>reservation</u>?**

   Ⓐ Re-

   Ⓑ Reserve

   ● -tion

   Ⓓ Reserving

4. **"The painting turned out to be <u>worth nothing</u>." Which word would best replace the underlined phrase?**

   ● Worthless

   Ⓑ Worthful

   Ⓒ Worthness

   Ⓓ Worthly

Lesson 3 — Common Word Roots and Bases

 **GETTING the IDEA**

Word roots are word parts that can be added to other word parts. Word roots hold the main meaning or definition of a word. If you know the meaning of the word root, you have a clue about what the whole word means.

Common Word Roots		
Root	**Meaning**	**Example**
-auto-	self	automobile, autograph
geo-	earth	geography, geology
multi-	many	multiply
tele-	far	telephone, telescope
vis-	see	vision, visible
bio-	life	biology, biosphere
-graph-	writing	autograph, graphic
-spec-	look, see	spectator, inspect
-port-	carry	transport, porter

You can combine common word roots to form new words.

auto + bio + graphy = autobiography

Auto- means "self." Bio- means "life." *Graph* means "writing." If you combine the meaning of each root, you form the word *autobiography.* An autobiography is writing about a person's life written by that person.

What other words can you form by combining word roots?

Prefixes and suffixes are groups of letters that cannot stand alone as whole words. Prefixes and suffixes are sometimes called **affixes** because they affix, or attach, themselves to words or other word parts. Unlike affixes, **base words** are real words that can stand alone. Prefixes and suffixes attach themselves to base words. When affixes attach to base words, word families form.

Look at these word families created by adding prefixes and suffixes to base words.

Base Word	Word Families
comfort	discomfort, uncomfortable, comforted, comforting
enjoy	enjoyment; enjoyable; enjoying; enjoyed
kind	unkind; kindness; kindly; kinder; kindest

Understanding an unfamiliar word is much easier if you break it down into its separate parts. First, what does the base word mean? Second, identify and define any prefixes or suffixes. Finally, combine the meaning of each word and word part. You will have the meaning of the unfamiliar word.

Let's look at the word *unusually*. Break the word down into its most basic parts.

Prefix	Base	Suffix
un-	usual	-ly

The prefix *un-* means "not." The word base *usual* means normal. The suffix *-ly* means "a characteristic of something." When you put all three of these parts together, you get a word that means having the characteristic of not being normal. In other words, unusually means something that does not commonly happen.

DISCUSS The telegraph was invented and used in the 1800s. What was the telegraph's purpose?

Try These

1. **What are you most likely to see if you look through a <u>telescope</u>?**

   Ⓐ Germs

   ● Stars

   Ⓒ People

   Ⓓ Bugs

   Tele- is a root that means "far." Which choice names an object that is located far away and would need a special tool to see it close up?

2. **What is a book called that is written about a person's life?**

   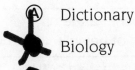 Dictionary

   ● Biology

   ● Biography

   Ⓓ Library

   Two of the answer choices have word roots that mean "life." Of those two choices, which one also has a root that means "written"?

3. **What do geologists study?**

   ● Earthquakes

   Ⓑ Electricity

   Ⓒ Life

   Ⓓ Bugs

4. **How many wheels are found on a tricycle?**

   Ⓐ 2

   ✗ 4

   Ⓒ 1

   ● 3

Lesson 4 Using Word Parts to Learn New Words

GETTING the IDEA Figuring out what new words mean is not hard. You just have to know how to separate the parts, know what they mean, and then put them back together again. Does it have a suffix? Does it have a prefix? Can you recognize the word root? Do you know what each part means? What happens when you add them all together?

When you add prefixes, suffixes, and roots to a word it can be difficult remembering what each part means. It is helpful to organize this information in a chart.

Break the following words into prefixes, suffixes, roots/bases:

disappeared, unkindness, regaining, irreversible

Prefix	Root/Base Word	Suffix
dis (means "not" or "away")	*appear* (means "to come into sight")	*ed* (means already happened")
un (means "not")	*kind* (means "nice" or "shows caring")	*ness* (means "state or condition of being")
re (means "again")	*gain* (means "to get or add something")	*ing* (shows that an action is taking place now)
ir (means "not")	*reverse* (means "to go backward")	*ible* (means "capable of being")

Once you break the word into parts, you can connect what each part means to find the meaning of the entire word.

When you speak, read, or write, start to think about these words as if they were broken down into parts. Breaking new words into parts makes them easier to understand. The more parts you know and understand, the more you can make sense out of new words.

Imagine that you are reading your health textbook and you come across this sentence:

Eating a large meal before going to bed can create some indigestion.

What happens if you do not know what *indigestion* means? Break it up into parts.

Prefix	Root	Suffix
in	digest	tion

Start with the prefix *in-*. The meaning of *in-* is "not." The suffix is *–tion*, an action or process. The root of the word is *digest*. D*igest* means "the breaking down of food for energy." When you put all three parts together, you can see that *indigestion* means "not being able to break down."

Let's try another one. If you were looking through a cookbook, you might see this sentence:

Keep some precooked *rice in the refrigerator to make some quick soups.*

What does *precooked* mean? Like before, break it into parts.

Prefix	Root	Suffix
pre	cook	ed

Start with the prefix *pre-*. The meaning *pre-* is "before." The root is *cook*. The suffix is *-ed*. This means "something that has happened in the past." Put it all together and you get "something that has already been cooked earlier."

NOTICE: Photocopying any part of this book is prohibited by law.

49

DISCUSS What is the base of *frightened*? What is the base of *swimming*? What is the base of *mistaken*? How do you find out which part is the base?

Try These

1. "The teacher <u>reviewed</u> the main points before we took the test." What does <u>reviewed</u> mean?

   → Ⓐ Took another look

   ⊗ Quizzed out loud

   ⊗ Will discuss tomorrow

   ⊗ Are going over now

   Remember, that the prefix *re-* means "to do again." The suffix *-ed* means it happened in the past. The base word *view* means "to look."

2. "Susan <u>overlooked</u> the fact that I was 15 minutes late." What does <u>overlooked</u> mean?

   ● Didn't notice

   Ⓑ Focused on

    Was thinking about

   Ⓓ Decided to ignore

   The prefix is *over-*. The root word is *look*. The suffix is *-ed*. Put them all together and you get someone looking past something.

3. "It was our fourth <u>disagreement</u> of the afternoon." What does <u>disagreement</u> mean?

   ● Argument

   Ⓑ Project

   Ⓒ Assignment

   Ⓓ Decision

4. "It is <u>unlikely</u> that I will get a dog for my birthday." What does <u>unlikely</u> mean?

   Ⓐ Probably going to happen

   Ⓑ Might happen

   ● Probably will not happen

   Ⓓ Unclear whether it will happen or not

Lesson

5   Compound Words

Compound words are made when two or more words are combined. For example, the compound word "doghouse" is made by joining the words "dog" and "house."

 + **=**

Compound words can be formed in one of three ways:

1. Joining two or more words to form one new word. These are sometimes called **closed compound words.** (birth + day = birthday)

2. Compound words can also be written as two separate words. These are sometimes called **open compound words**. (home + team = home team)

3. Some compound words are joined by hyphens. These are sometimes called **hyphenated compound words.** (sister + in + law = sister-in-law)

Common Compound Words			
airplane	anyone	birthday	bedroom
cardboard	cupboard	daylight	eyeball
everyday	fingerprint	fireman	goldfish
handwriting	indoors	inside	landmark
looking-glass	merry-go-round	myself	overuse
post office	today	update	well-being
waterfall	viewpoint	space shuttle	living-room

How many compound words can you form by joining the following words?

court	back	home	house	work	team	tennis	pack	yard

Read this passage. Find examples of open, closed, and hyphenated compound words in the passage while you read.

SEBASTIAN FOR PRESIDENT

"Do not forget, anyone who wants to run for class president should add his or her name to the sign-up sheet. There are sign-up sheets on the bulletin board at the back of the room," said Mrs. O'Leary.

Sebastian had big plans for how he could make life in fourth grade more fun. He walked to the bulletin board and added his name to the list. When he returned to his seat, his mind began to wander. Mrs. O'Leary's voice faded into the background. Sebastian drifted deeper and deeper into his <u>daydream</u>.

"I am excited to tell you that our next class president won by a landslide! This amazing boy got twenty-five votes. Congratulations go to…Sebastian!"

His fantasy continued. Sebastian dreamed of his classmates cheering. Then they headed to the parking lot for a parade. In his dream, Sebastian sat on top of a fire engine. His best friend Ryan was elected vice president. Ryan was sitting next to him. Sebastian and Ryan waved as the fire engine drove around the schoolyard.

"Sebastian…Sebastian!"

Sebastian was startled back into reality at the sound of Mrs. O'Leary calling his name.

Learning about compound words can help you to become a better reader. Sometimes   you can use what you know about the parts of a compound word to help you figure out its meaning. Find the word daydream in the story above. What does this word mean?

Other times, you need more than what you know about the parts of a compound word to figure out its meaning. When this happens, look for clues in the story or use a dictionary to find the meaning of the compound word.

DISCUSS   What compound words can you think of that have to deal with school?

Try These

1. **Which word means "a building for plants to grow in"?**

   Ⓐ Skyscraper

   Ⓑ Homework

   Ⓒ Greenhouse

   Ⓓ Planter

   Separate each compound word into two words. Think about what each separated word means. Now think about what they mean as one word, when you put them back together.

2. **Which word means "a storm in which a lot of snow falls"?**

   Ⓐ Snow-white

   Ⓑ Snowstorm

   Ⓒ Snowshoe

   Ⓓ Snowmobile

   Although each choice's compound word begins with the word "snow," only one choice means "a storm in which a lot of snow falls." Look at the second word part of each compound word choice. Which one means "a lot of snow falling"?

3. **What is a courtroom?**

   Ⓐ A room where the proceedings of a court are held.

   Ⓑ A lounge area for lawyers.

   Ⓒ The location of more than one basketball court.

   Ⓓ The building where the proceedings of a court are held.

    Write your answer on a separate sheet of paper. Write your answer in complete sentences. Use the Extended Response Reading Rubric on page 81 to help you write your answer.

4. **Think of the school items that you named that were examples of compound words. Write a short paragraph using at least four of these words. Use information from the lesson and your own ideas to support your answer.**

Read Part 1 of "The Lost Lake" which describes a father and son's summer camping adventure.

THE LOST LAKE
by Allen Say

I went to live with Dad last summer.

Every day he worked in his room from morning to night, sometimes on weekends, too. Dad wasn't much of a talker, but when he was busy he didn't talk at all.

I didn't know anybody in the city, so I stayed home most of the time. It was too hot to play outside anyway. In one month I finished all the books I'd brought and grew tired of watching TV.

One morning I started cutting pictures out of old magazines, just to be doing something. They were pictures of mountains and rivers and lakes, and some showed people fishing and canoeing. Looking at them made me feel cool, so I pinned them up in my room.

Dad didn't notice them for two days. When he did, he looked at them one by one. "Nice pictures," he said.

"Are you angry with me, Dad?" I asked, because he saved old magazines for his work.

"It's all right, Luke," he said. "I'm having this place painted soon anyway." He thought I was talking about the marks I'd made on the wall.

That Saturday Dad woke me up early in the morning and told me we were going camping! I was wide awake in a second. He gave me a pair of brand-new hiking boots to try out. They were perfect.

In the hallway I saw a big backpack and a knapsack all packed and ready to go. "What's in them, Dad?" I asked.

"Later," he said. "We have a long drive ahead of us."

In the car I didn't ask any more questions because Dad was so grumpy in the morning.

"Where are we going?" I finally asked.

`We're off to the Lost Lake, my lad."

"How can you lose a lake?"

"No one's found it, that's how." Dad was smiling! "Grandpa and I used to go there a long time ago. It was our special place, so don't tell any of your friends."

"I'll never tell," I promised. "How long are we going to stay there?"

"Five days, maybe a week."

"We're going to sleep outside for a whole week?"

"That's the idea."

"Oh, boy!"

We got to the mountains in the afternoon.

1. **Which word has a suffix?**

    (A) People

    (B) Saturday

    (C) Backpack

    (D) Hiking

    1.A.1a; 1.A.2a/1.4.01   Suffixes

2. **If you add the prefix im- to perfect, what does the new word mean?**

    (A) Not perfect

    (B) Extra perfect

    (C) Used to be perfect

    (D) Perfect again

    1.A.1a; 1.A.2a/1.4.01   Prefixes

3. **Which of these words is a compound word?**

    (A) Stayed

    (B) Mountains

    (C) Weekends

    (D) Questions

    1.A.1b; 1.A.2a/1.4.03   Compound Words

4. **What does the suffix –ly mean in the word finally?**

    (A) A characteristic of

    (B) Against

    (C) Once again

    (D) In the process of

    1.A.1a; 1.A.2a/1.4.01   Suffixes

5. **What does the word <u>hallway</u> mean?**

   Ⓐ A passageway between rooms

   Ⓑ The door into a basement or attic

   Ⓒ The front entry to a home or apartment

   Ⓓ A way to get from one floor to another

   1.A.1b; 1.A.2a/1.4.03   Compound Words

6. **What is the word root of <u>canoeing</u>?**

   Ⓐ Can

   Ⓑ Noe

   Ⓒ Canoe

   Ⓓ Ing

   1.A.1b; 1.A.2a/1.4.02; 1.4.27 Word Roots

7. **Which word has a suffix?**

   Ⓐ Finished

   Ⓑ Place

   Ⓒ Mug

   Ⓓ Coffee

   1.A.1a; 1.A.2a/1.4.01   Suffixes

8. **What is the suffix in <u>irreversible</u>?**

   Ⓐ Ir-

   Ⓑ Re-

   Ⓒ Reverse

   Ⓓ -ible

   1.A.1a; 1.A.2a/1.4.01   Suffixes

9. **Which word has the same meaning as <u>grumpy</u>?**

   Ⓐ Funny

   Ⓑ Strange

   Ⓒ Confusing

   Ⓓ Crabby

   1.A.1b; 1.A.2a/1.4.05   Synonyms

10. **Which word means the opposite of <u>notice</u>?**

   Ⓐ Remember

   Ⓑ Dislike

   Ⓒ Ignore

   Ⓓ Discuss

   1.A.1b; 1.A.2a/1.4.06   Antonyms

Lesson 6 — Using Context Clues

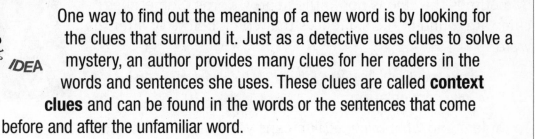

GETTING the IDEA

One way to find out the meaning of a new word is by looking for the clues that surround it. Just as a detective uses clues to solve a mystery, an author provides many clues for her readers in the words and sentences she uses. These clues are called **context clues** and can be found in the words or the sentences that come before and after the unfamiliar word.

A context clue can be a definition, an example, a synonym, or an antonym. The chart below shows some of the ways that an author can give clues to readers. The words in *italics* may be unfamiliar to you. The underlined words are clues that hint at the meaning of the unknown word.

Type of Context Clue	Example
Definition	He sold me a *pomegranate*, a tart, seed-filled fruit.
Example	She was a *mystic*, like Merlin or the witches of Endor.
Synonym or Antonym	That is a *blessed*, or sacred, place.

Sometimes context clues are found in the same sentences as the unfamiliar word. For example, look at this sentence:

The entire audience began clapping loudly the moment the concert ended.

If you did not know what the word *audience* meant, you can figure out its meaning by looking at the words around it. Let's look at the clues. From the sentence, you know that the audience is clapping. You also know that the audience is watching a concert. Who or what goes to concerts and can clap? The word *entire* lets you know that you are talking about more than one person. Those clues could lead you to what the word *audience* means—a group of listeners.

Here is another example.

> *"Class, may I have your attention? Please read pages 1–5 as part of your <u>assignment</u> for tonight," Mrs. Ward said at the end of class. "Then answer the reading questions."*

Look at the rest of the sentence surrounding the word *assignment*. The clues in the sentence tell you that a teacher gives an assignment for the whole class. From this you can figure out that an *assignment* was what the teacher gave out for homework.

Sometimes the clue is not in the nearby words. Sometimes clues are found in the sentences that come before or after the word.

> *Elaine and Carol had been talking on the phone for hours. It was a long <u>conversation</u>.*

To understand what *conversation* means you have to look beyond the sentence the unknown word is in. In this example, the clues are found in the first sentence. It shows that two people have been talking on the phone for a long time. You can see that *conversation* means people talking together.

Sometimes, you may come across a word that has multiple meanings. You may have to think about what the story is about. For example, look at this sentence:

> *Kevin could not believe it. He had actually gotten a <u>strike</u>! It was his first one.*

Before you know whether to feel good or bad for Kevin, you have to figure out what kind of strike it is. Is it a strike in baseball? That's not good. Is it a strike in bowling? That's very good. Be sure to pay attention to the setting of the story (a baseball field or a bowling alley) and use it as an extra clue for understanding new words.

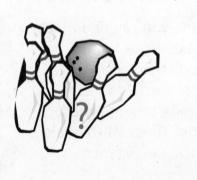
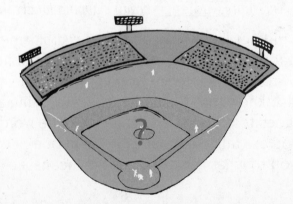

DISCUSS How can the setting of a story help you to understand unfamiliar words?

Try These

Use context clues to determine the meaning of each underlined word.

1. **Sheila had a huge <u>collection</u>. There were bears on her shelves, on her bed and on her floor.**

   Ⓐ A group or set of bears

   Ⓑ A large book about bears

   A big stuffed bear on the bed

   Movies about polar bears

Find clues that surround the word. *Huge* tells you that a collection is big. The next sentence gives a clue about what is found in the collection.

---

2. **It was raining hard. The wind was fierce. The weather was truly <u>dreadful</u>.**

   Ⓐ Freezing

   Ⓑ Confusing

   ● Terrible

   Ⓓ Curious

3. **The young girl was an <u>expert</u> on horses. She had studied and worked with horses since she was five, and could get her horse to do tricks without ever making a mistake.**

   Ⓐ A full time horse trainer

   ● A person who knows a lot about something

   Ⓒ A person who teaches horseback riding

   Ⓓ A professional horse racer

Look at the clues that describe what the girl did to become an expert.

---

4. **The police waited for the thief. They expected him to return to the <u>scene</u> of the crime.**

   A small piece or part of a play

    The place where something happened

   Ⓒ Have watched or witnessed an event

   Ⓓ A thief's hideout

Lesson 7

Synonyms

GETTING the IDEA

Synonyms are words that have the same or almost the same meaning. Sometimes when you write or speak, you may find yourself saying the same word over and over. There are so many other exciting and fun words that can be used.

Look at this example:

I had a lot of fun at your house the other day. Making cookies was fun. Of course, eating them was even more fun.

Even though you had a good time doing all of those things, there are other words to use than *fun*. Knowing some of them can make what you say more interesting. It can also make your writing stronger and more exciting.

Synonyms	
happy	glad, pleased, joyful, cheery, lucky, content
answer	reply, respond, react, solve, lay to rest
say	declare, state, announce, say, speak out, proclaim
eat	gobble, gulp, munch, swallow, chew, consume
great	wonderful, excellent, terrific, good, cool, fantastic

Using the Right Synonym

Synonyms give you different ways to express yourself. Be careful though! Although synonyms are words that are similar in meaning, some synonyms work better than others depending on how they are used in a sentence.

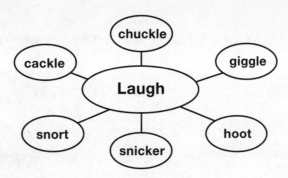

Look at the word *laugh*. Then look at the words on the lines. Each one means almost the same thing. How are they different? Each one describes a different kind of laugh.

- For example, you might use *chuckle*, a loud, happy laugh, for when your friend tells you a good joke at lunch time.
- You might use *giggle*, a soft, gentle laugh, for when your little sister does something cute at the dinner table.
- An explosive *hoot* is just right for a funny moment on your favorite television show.
- A *snort* is done more with your nose than your mouth and is just right for that unexpected funny line from a teacher.

These small differences can mean a lot in your writing and speaking. Be careful when choosing which synonym to use in writing or speaking. You want to make sure you are saying exactly what you meant to say.

Example

Choose the best synonym for the following sentences.

The dog _____ through the park right on the squirrel's tail.

Ⓐ Walked

Ⓑ Hiked

Ⓒ Raced

Ⓓ Marched

Think about the picture the writer or speaker wants you to see with this sentence. "To walk" means to take your time. "To hike" means a strong walk with a goal in mind. "To race" shows that someone is in a hurry (which he is if chasing a squirrel). "To march" is to move with a beat. The words you choose are the ones that will paint a picture in your reader's mind.

Try thinking of words as colors. Imagine you are painting a picture with them. Make sure that you choose the right shade— or synonym—to paint the exact picture you want.

Think of synonyms for the word *funny*. When would it be appropriate to use each?

Try These

1. **Which synonym best completes this sentence? "The large _____ had room enough for at least sixty people."**

   Ⓐ Cottage

    Studio

   Ⓒ Shack

   ● House

   Look at the clues in the sentence. What would be big enough to fit sixty people?

2. **Which synonym best completes this sentence? "The _____ little girl screamed and could not stop shaking after her brother jumped out of her closet wearing a scary mask."**

    Scared

   Worried

   Terrified

   Nervous

   Think about the amount of fear the little girl felt when she saw the masked figure come from her closet. Which word shows the greatest fear?

3. **Which of the following words is not a synonym of <u>favorite</u>?**

   Ⓐ Treasured

   Ⓑ Adored

    Disliked

   Ⓓ Loved

    Write your answer on a separate sheet of paper. Write your answer in complete sentences. Use the Extended Response Reading Rubric on page 81 to help you write your answer.

4. **The word <u>break</u> has many synonyms, such as <u>smash</u>, <u>rupture</u>, <u>shatter</u>, <u>crack</u> or <u>split</u>. Describe how each one might be used. How are they different? Use information from the lesson and your own ideas to support your answer.**

Lesson 8 Antonyms

Antonyms are words that are the opposite of synonyms. Instead of having the same meaning as another word, an antonym has the opposite meaning.

Antonyms	
fast	slow
laugh	cry
day	night
asleep	awake
light	dark
cute	ugly
enemy	friend
safe	dangerous
east	west
forget	remember

Use the chart to identify each pair of antonyms shown in the pictures below.

Antonyms can be used as context clues to help readers understand the meaning of unfamiliar words.

Example

What does *modest* mean in the sentence, "Unlike Julie who was proud and liked to brag, Rose was *modest*"?

Ⓐ Humble

Ⓑ Prideful

Ⓒ Mean

Ⓓ Conceited

First look at the word *proud*. What qualities does a proud person show? Pride causes people to brag about their achievements. Proud people like everyone to know how great they are. A modest person would do the opposite. A modest person would keep his or her accomplishments to himself or herself, which is humble.

Antonyms can also be used to make comparisons or to show differences.

Although Colleen was only a <u>child</u>, she spoke with the wisdom of an <u>adult</u>.

What do the antonyms in this sentence emphasize about Colleen?

First think about how adults and children are different. Life experiences teach wisdom. The older you get, the more life experiences you will have. This should teach you wisdom. Think about what information the antonyms give. You know that Colleen is a young girl. In the sentence, the antonym stresses how unlike a child Colleen is.

Read the paragraph below. Fill in the chart by pairing antonyms found in this paragraph.

Unlike her own mother who was very <u>kind</u> and loving, Cinderella's stepmother was <u>cruel</u>. She made poor Cinderella sleep in the <u>cold</u> attic while she slept in the <u>warmth</u> under a stack of thick blankets in a room with a fireplace. One of the many jobs Cinderella had was to <u>neatly</u> make the beds without any wrinkles. Cinderella's stepmother often made Cinderella remake the beds, insisting that they were sloppily made.

Antonym Pairs	
kind	
cold	
neatly	

DISCUSS How can antonyms be used to make comparisons?

Try These

1. **Which antonym best completes this sentence? "Kathy loves strawberries as much as she _____ cucumbers."**

    (A) Enjoys

    (B) Appreciates

    (C) Hates

    (D) Avoids

2. **Which antonym best completes this sentence? "The elephant was so huge that it made the bear in the next cage look _____."**

    (A) Fierce

    (B) Sad

    (C) Angry

    (D) Tiny

3. **Which set of words are antonyms?**

    (A) Warm/Cozy

    (B) Warm/Hot

    (C) Warm/Cool

    (D) Cool/Hip

 Write your answer on a separate sheet of paper. Write your answer in complete sentences. Use the Extended Response Reading Rubric on page 81 to help you write your answer.

4. **List an antonym for each of the following words:**

    mine famous buy less inside open first nice hide

    Use information from the lesson and your own ideas to support your answer.

Lesson 9 Homonyms, Homophones, and Homographs

It is easy to confuse words that look or sound alike but mean different things. **Homonyms** are words that sound the same and often have the same spelling, but have different meanings. **Homophones** are words that sound the same but have different spellings and different meanings. **Homographs** are words that have the same spelling but different meanings and (sometimes) different pronunciations.

It is important to know the difference between homonyms, homophones, and homographs—and then make sure you use the right one in the right place. If you use the wrong one, it can make your writing confusing.

Homonyms	
row (rhymes with slow; means a layer; My seat was in the first <u>row</u>.)	**row** (rhymes with slow; to move with oars; <u>Row, row, row</u> your boat)
grave (rhymes with brave; a burial place; We put flowers on the <u>grave</u>.)	**grave** (rhymes with brave; solemn or serious; When Dad looked at my report card, he had a <u>grave</u> look on his face.)
hide (rhymes with side; to put or keep secret or out of sight; I <u>hide</u> my journal so my sister doesn't read what I wrote.)	**hide** (rhymes with side; the skin of an animal; The teepee was made of buffalo <u>hide</u>.)

Homophones	
allowed (to have permission; I am <u>allowed</u> to go to the party.)	**aloud** (with a speaking voice; orally; Please read the story <u>aloud</u>.)
bear (a large, furry animal; <u>Bears</u> hibernate in winter.)	**bare** (lacking clothing; Her feet were <u>bare</u> without socks and shoes.)
their (showing possession; belonging to more than one person; The girls took <u>their</u> pets to the park.)	**they're; there** (they are; place; <u>They're</u> going over <u>there</u> to play on the swings.)
blew (past tense of blow; Scott <u>blew</u> out the candles on his birthday cake.)	**blue** (a color; Ryan painted his bedroom <u>blue</u> and yellow.)
know (to grasp or understand; I <u>know</u> how to make a paper airplane.)	**no** (the opposite of yes; My mom said <u>no</u> when I asked if I could get a dog.)
sent (to direct or allow to leave; I was <u>sent</u> home from school when I was sick.)	**cent** (a form of money; I was given 50 <u>cents</u> to buy a pack of gum.)

Scent

Homographs	
bass (rhymes with class; a fish; I went <u>bass</u> fishing with my uncle.)	**bass** (rhymes with place; producing a low tone; I play the <u>bass</u> guitar in the band.)
bow (rhymes with so; The present was tied with a <u>bow</u>.)	**bow** (rhymes with cow; to lower oneself to show honor; <u>Bow</u> down before meeting royalty.)
tear (rhymes with clear; what is released when you cry; A <u>tear</u> rolled down his cheek when he realized his dog had run away.)	**tear** (rhymes with hair; to rip; He had a <u>tear</u> in his shirt.)
dove (rhymes with love; a bird; A white <u>dove</u> is the symbol for purity.)	**dove** (rhymes with stove; to dip; She <u>dove</u> for the ball and got the runner out.)

Example 1

Read this sentence. Can you spot the error?

The <u>male</u> is put in the <u>mail</u>box everyday at noon.
    1   2

Male and mail are homophones. A *male* refers to a boy or a man. *Mail* is something that is delivered by the postal carrier via the post office.

Example 2

Read this sentence. How is the homonym set used in each?

Please <u>set</u> the table. Please use the matching <u>set</u> of blue dishes.
    1   2

In the first example, *set* means "to place." In the second example, *set* means "a part of a matching group."

Example 3

Read these sentences. How is the homograph *wind* used in each?

<u>Wind</u> up the toy duck by turning the knob in the back. See how it waddles?
   1

A strong <u>wind</u> blew and knocked over the flowerpot.
            2

In the first example, *wind* means "to turn again and again." In the second example, *wind* is the movement of air.

DISCUSS Why is it possible that, when you use the spell check function on your computer, your paper might still contain errors?

Try These

1. Which word best completes this sentence? "They are going to _____ house for the afternoon."

   (A) They're

   (B) Their

   (C) There

   (D) They are

   Choice A is a contraction for "they are" and would not work in the sentence. Choice C is a location and Choice D is the same as Choice A.

2. Which word will best complete this sentence? "The science paper is _____ on Monday."

   (A) Due

   (B) Do

   (C) Dew

   (D) Done

   Choice B is a verb in the wrong form for this sentence. Choice C is a noun. Choice D is not part of the homonyms.

3. Which word best completes this sentence? "The _____ of the cookies in the oven made my stomach growl."

   (A) Sent

   (B) Cent

   (C) Scent

   (D) Send

4. Which sentence contains a pair of homographs?

   (A) Everyone on board felt bored.

   (B) The miner made a minor mistake.

   (C) He wound a scarf around the wound.

   (D) We rode a wagon down the road.

NOTICE: Photocopying any part of this book is prohibited by law.

69

Unit 1 Review

> The following passage is from the book *Stuart Little* by E. B. White. It is a story about a mouse named Stuart who walks and talks just like a human. He even has a human family!

THE DRAIN

When Mrs. Frederick C. Little's second son arrived, everybody noticed that he was not much bigger than a mouse. The truth of the matter was, the baby looked very much like a mouse in every way. He was only about two inches high; and he had a mouse's sharp nose, a mouse's tail, a mouse's whiskers, and the pleasant, shy manner of a mouse. Before he was many days old he was not only looking like a mouse but acting like one, too—wearing a gray hat and carrying a small cane. Mr. and Mrs. Little named him Stuart, and Mr. Little made him a tiny bed out of four clothespins and a tiny box.

Unlike most babies, Stuart could walk as soon as he was born. When he was a week old he could climb lamps by shimmying up the cord. Mrs. Little saw right away that the infant clothes she had provided were unsuitable, and she set to work and made him a fine little blue worsted suit with patch pockets in which he could keep his handkerchief, his money, and his keys. Every morning, before Stuart dressed, Mrs. Little went into his room and weighed him on a small scale which was really meant for weighing letters. At birth Stuart could have been sent by first class mail for three cents, but his parents preferred to keep him rather than send him away; and when, at the age of a month, he had gained only a third of an ounce, his mother was so worried she sent for the doctor.

The doctor was delighted with Stuart and said that it was very unusual for an American family to have a mouse. He took Stuart's temperature and found that is was 98.6, which is normal for a mouse. He also examined Stuart's chest and heart and looked into his ears solemnly with a flashlight. (Not every doctor can look into a mouse's ear without laughing.) Everything seemed to be all right, and Mrs. Little was pleased to get such a good report.

"Feed him up!" said the doctor cheerfully, as he left.

The home of the Little family was a pleasant place near a park in New York City. In the mornings the sun streamed in through the east windows, and all the Littles were up early as a general rule. Stuart was a great help to his parents, and to his older brother, George, because of his small size and because he could do things that a mouse can do and was agreeable about doing them. One day when Mrs. Little was washing out the bathtub after Mr. Little had taken a bath, she lost a ring off her finger and was horrified to discover that it had fallen down the drain.

"What had I better do?" she cried, trying to keep the tears back.

"If I were you" said George "I should bend a hair in the shape of a fishhook and tie it onto a piece of string and try to fish the ring out with it. So Mrs. Little found a piece of string and a hairpin, and for about a half-hour she fished for the ring; but it was dark down the drain and the hook always seemed to catch on something before she could get it down to where the ring was.

1. Which word contains a suffix?

- Ⓐ Something
- Ⓑ Cheerfully
- Ⓒ Unusual
- Ⓓ Manner

1.A.1a/1.4.01   Suffixes

2. Which word is a synonym of pleasant?

- Ⓐ Unfriendly
- Ⓑ Lazy
- Ⓒ Enjoyable
- Ⓓ Smart

1.A.1b; 1.A.2a/1.4.05   Synonyms

3. What does the word root tele- mean in telegram?

- Ⓐ Write
- Ⓑ Life
- Ⓒ Distant
- Ⓓ Books

1.A.1a; 1.A.2a/1.4.01   Word Roots

4. What is the word root of destruction?

- Ⓐ De
- Ⓑ Struct
- Ⓒ Destruct
- Ⓓ Tion

1.A.1a; 1.A.2a/1.4.01   Word Roots

5. Which of the following is a compound word?

Ⓐ Examine

Ⓑ Refrigerator

Ⓒ Discover

Ⓓ Flashlight

1.A.1b; 1.A.2a/1.4.03   Compound Words

6. Which word is a synonym of unusual?

Ⓐ Strange

Ⓑ Common

Ⓒ Bright

Ⓓ Expensive

1.A.1b; 1.A.2b/1.4.05   Synonyms

7. Which word is an antonym of general?

Ⓐ Usual

Ⓑ Common

Ⓒ Specific

Ⓓ Shared

1.A.1b; 1.A.2b/1.4.06   Antonyms

8. The doctor "also examined Stuart's chest and heart and looked into his ears solemnly with a flashlight. (Not every doctor can look into a mouse's ear without laughing)." What does the word solemn mean?

Ⓐ Serious

Ⓑ Angry

Ⓒ Funny

Ⓓ Sad

1.A.1b; 1.A.2b/1.4.04; 1.4.07   Using Context Clues

9. Which sentence uses a homonym correctly?

Ⓐ Stuart had a mouse's tale and a mouse's sharp nose.

Ⓑ He was only about two inches high.

Ⓒ Mrs. Little's wring fell down the drain.

Ⓓ Stuart is Mrs. Little's second sun.

1.A.2a/1.4.08   Homonyms

Now I Can...

Use the skills checklist below to help you complete the "Now I Can . . ." statements.

Now that I know the meanings of common _____, _____, and _____, I can connect what I know about these word parts to determine the meaning of unknown words.

Now that I know how to use _____ _____, I can connect these clues to determine the word that best fits a given sentence.

Now that I know what a _____ _____ is, I can tell that the word *homework* is made by joining the words *home* and *work*.

...Make the Connection

Place a check in the box indicating the skill you've mastered.

These are the skills I've learned in this unit:

☐ Prefixes

☐ Suffixes

☐ Common Word Roots

☐ Using Word Parts to Learn New Words

☐ Compound Words

☐ Using Context Clues

☐ Synonyms

☐ Antonyms

☐ Homonyms

Reading Strategies

Have you ever played a game like chess or checkers? If so, you know that if you want to win, there are certain strategies that you can use. Strategies are plans of action that can help you complete a task. You can use strategies when you read as well. Sometimes ideas are very clear, or **explicit**. Other times, you may have to look harder because these ideas are indirect, or less clear, or **implied**.

Even if you have not seen or heard what the characters in the story are doing, most of the time you can still understand the story because of your prior knowledge. **Prior knowledge** includes all the facts, details, and ideas that you have learned from life—your family, school, friends, books, or television.

You will learn how to **make predictions** about a passage. You do this by guessing what is going to happen next by using the clues in the text. Making predictions can make a passage easier to understand.

You learn from everything you read, whether it be a poem, a story, or an article. **Making comparisons across passages** will help you understand how different types of literature can be useful for learning new information. By reading two different kinds of writing about the same topic, you can often learn even more.

Graphic organizers can help you see and better understand main ideas. You can organize information in a text by making a list, a diagram, or a chart.

Try This

Separate into groups of three or four. You will need paper, pencil, and a textbook.

- Think of something you have recently learned in one of your classes. List the main ideas of what the lesson was about. Discuss whether you think the ideas were stated clearly or if you had to work to figure them out. Does everyone agree on what was clear and what wasn't? Some ideas might seem clear to some people and unclear to others.

- Discuss what a mystery book or movie is like. Talk about how you can find clues in either one. How does the detective use these clues to solve the mystery? Discuss how you can be like a detective when you read. What information or clues did you have that helped you make your prediction?

Lesson 10 Writing Extended-Response Answers

GETTING the IDEA

Extended-response questions appear on the ISAT test. These questions require you to write a response instead of selecting a multiple-choice answer. This type of question also requires students to do the following: be good readers, identify important information in the text, use prior knowledge to make a text connection, and balance the author's ideas with their own. This lesson will help you develop the skills you will need to answer extended-response questions.

Read this passage from *Spider* magazine. Notice how a student has taken notes. These notes show how the student was thinking about the passage and preparing to write about it.

THE CRACKED CHINESE JUG

by Carolyn Han

1   Each morning Han Han fetched water for his village from the river. He placed a bamboo shoulder pole across his back and put the empty jugs on either side.

2   When Han Han returned to the village, he had one and a half jugs of water. One clay jar had a tiny crack, and some of its water had leaked out.

3   The perfect jug was *proud* of itself. It had carried a full load of water. But the imperfect jug was *embarrassed.* It had done only half of the work.

Han Han carries water. He must live in a small village without modern conveniences.

Why doesn't he care that water is lost?

Contrast between jugs!

4   One day the cracked jug could stand it no longer. "I'm a failure," it cried. "Why do I have a crack?"

5   Ignoring the jug's cry, Han Han carefully filled both jugs with water at the river. By the time they reached the village, the cracked jug was only half full. "Why don't you throw me away?" asked the broken jug.

6   Han Han smiled at the jugs and put them on the shelf.   *Why does he smile?*

7   The next morning when Han Han placed the jugs on the ends of his shoulder pole; he said to the broken one, "For months I've heard you complain."   *Is Han Han mad?*

8   "I'm ashamed of myself," answered the cracked jug. "I'm worthless."   *Strong words!*

9   "Today when we return to the village, I want you to look along the path," said Han Han.   *Strange comment!*

10   It was the first time the broken jug noticed the flowers. The colorful flowers made the cracked jug very happy. But then it remembered its crack and the leaking water, and again it felt sad.

11   "What did you think of the flowers?" asked Han Han.   *!*

12   "They're pretty," replied the jug. "They're only growing on my side of the path."

13   "That's right," said Han Han. "For months you've watered the wildflower seeds. Your 'failure,' as you call it, has changed our village and made it more beautiful."   *WOW!*

14   "Then all that time I felt useless," said the cracked jug, "my flaw was really my most valuable part!"   *Lesson!*

Reading The Question

If this passage were on the ISAT, this is one example of an extended-response question that you would be expected to answer.

What lesson did the writer want readers to learn by reading the story? Use information from the story and your own ideas to support your answer.

Look at the question and read it over several times. Think about what it means. Break it up into its parts:

Part 1: What lesson did the writer of this story want readers to learn by reading the story?

Say to yourself: *This tells me that I have to tell what the lesson is in the story. I need to go back and look for the lesson.*

Part 2: Use information from the story and from what you know already to explain your answer.

Say to yourself: *This means that I have to tell about what I learned from the story as I write my answer. I also should use what I already know about the lesson in my answer.*

Looking For Ideas

Now **read the passage again**, looking for ideas that will help you answer it. If you are allowed to write in the test booklet, **make notes** that will help you. **Circle or underline words and phrases that will help you**.

If you have extra paper, you can take notes on it, too. You can **use the notes to help you write.**

NOTICE: Photocopying any part of this book is prohibited by law.

A Sample Answer

Here is how Carla started to work with this question.

1. **What lesson did the writer of this story want readers to learn from reading the story?** See last paragraph: Sometimes our flaws are more valuable than we think.

2. **Use information from the story and make a connection to what you already know to explain your answer.**

<u>From the story:</u> Retell parts about how the cracked jug feels bad about itself, and how the uncracked jug makes it feel bad. Then show that the jug feels better when it finds out that the water it lost went to a good use.

<u>What I already knew:</u> People sometimes are upset with themselves. They think that they have faults. Sometimes those faults can be useful, like the cracked jug's leak.

Here is the answer Carla wrote using these notes:

The lesson that I think that the writer wanted readers to learn from the story is that we should not worry about our faults. We should just be what we are. In the story, the cracked jug was always calling itself a failure and worrying about the water that it lost. It let the perfect jug make it feel bad. What the cracked jug did not realize was that the crack was not a fault. The crack was a good thing, because it helped the water get to the flower seeds, so flowers could grow.

I think that this is a useful lesson because it can be used by many people. For example, my little brother feels bad because he is short. However, he was the only person who was small enough to get into a cupboard to get out something that my mother needed. His height was a useful quality then, like the jar's crack.

Analysis of Carla's Answer

There are some things to notice about this response. It begins by retelling the question and gives a clear lesson that is part of the story. It retells parts of the story that relate to the lesson.

In the second paragraph, Carla includes a specific example from her life to show where someone's fault was actually a useful quality, like the crack in the jar.

Notice that Carla uses information from the story (in the first paragraph) as well as information from real life (in the second paragraph). In this way, she has done what was asked of her in the last part of the question.

Checking Your Answer

The teachers who will be grading your written questions will be checking them against a scoring guide called a rubric. You can find a similar guide on page 81.

Make sure you explain ideas and information from the passage. You must also connect your own ideas or tell things from real life that relate to the question. Include information that will explain your answer.

You must also make certain that your writing has as few mistakes as possible. Here is a checklist that will help you find any errors and correct them.

- ☐ Have you read the question carefully?
- ☐ Have you planned your answer carefully?
- ☐ Have you stated the question in your answer?
- ☐ Have you supported your answer with examples and important details from the text?
- ☐ Have you supported your answer with information from your own experiences?
- ☐ Have you connected your ideas to the author's ideas?
- ☐ Have you answered all parts of the question?
- ☐ Is the response written in complete sentences?
- ☐ Have you explained the main idea from the text?
- ☐ Is the capitalization and punctuation correct?
- ☐ Are the words spelled correctly?
- ☐ Can a reader understand your writing?

Student-Friendly Extended-Response Reading Rubric

SCORE	CRITERIA
4	<ul><li>I explain the main ideas and important information from the text.</li><li>I connect my own ideas or experiences to the author's ideas.</li><li>I use examples and important details to support my answer.</li><li>I balance the author's ideas with my own ideas.</li></ul>
3	<ul><li>I explain some of the main ideas and important information from the text.</li><li>I connect some of my own ideas or experiences to the author's ideas.</li><li>I use some examples and important details to support my answer.</li><li>I balance only some of the author's ideas with my own ideas.</li></ul>
2	<ul><li>I explain only a few ideas from the text.</li><li>I summarize the text without including any of my own ideas or experiences</li></ul> OR <ul><li>I explain my own ideas without explaining the text.</li><li>I use general statements instead of specific details and examples.</li></ul>
1	<ul><li>I explain little or nothing from the text.</li><li>I use incorrect or unimportant information from the text.</li><li>I write too little to show I understand the text.</li></ul>
0	<ul><li>I write nothing.</li><li>I do not respond to the task.</li></ul>

Try These

Write your answer on a separate sheet of paper. Write your answer in complete sentences. Use the Extended Response Reading Rubric on page 81 to help you write your answer.

1. What do you think the uncracked jug will say when it sees the flowers and hears the praise that the cracked jug receives? Use information from the passage and your own ideas to support your answer.

2. Why doesn't Han Han get rid of the jug or fix it when it complains? Use information from the story and your own ideas to support your answer.

Lesson 11

Identify Explicit and Implied Idea

GETTING the IDEA

When authors write a story, article, or poem, they include many different ideas in it. Some of those ideas are **explicit**, or very obvious. You can't miss them. Others are implied, or not as clear. **Implied** ideas hint at something that you must figure out by combining information from the text and prior knowledge.

Here is an example:

The baby chicks ran in every direction, and I knew I was in trouble.

What explicit ideas are in this sentence? What ideas are implied?

Here is another example:

The class cheered when they heard the announcement about the weather.

What explicit ideas are in this sentence? What ideas are implied?

Explicit	Implied
The baby chicks are running around and the person is in trouble.	Someone might have forgotten to close the gate. The chicks might be in danger.
There is a class, and the students are happy about the announcement they just heard.	Perhaps a blizzard is coming and school is being canceled for the rest of the day.

NOTICE: Photocopying any part of this book is prohibited by law.

83

Read the next paragraph. Can you figure out what the main idea is? Is the main idea explicit or is it implied?

Example 1

The small shovel, flower seeds, and watering can were set out on the ground. My uncle put two bags of dirt next to me. He pulled on a pair of gloves and handed a pair to me. "Let's get started," he said. This was going to be fun.

What is the story going to be about? Is the idea explicit or implied?

Think about what the two people in the story are doing. What is going to be fun? Where do you think the story will go from here? The person and his or her uncle are about to begin gardening. In this case, the idea was implied. The word *garden* is not even mentioned. By using the explicit story clues, you can figure out the main idea.

This chart lists the explicit and implied ideas in Example 1.

Explicit	Implied
• The person and his or her uncle have a small shovel, flower seeds, and a watering can.	• The person and his or her uncle are going to begin gardening.
• The uncle pulled on a pair of gloves and handed a pair to his nephew/niece. • They have two bags of dirt.	• They are going to plant some flowers. • They do not want to get their hands dirty.

Example 2

The bank opened at 9:00 A.M. that morning, and I was the first one through the front door. I had been waiting for this for months. I could not wait to open my own account.

What is this story going to be about? Is the idea explicit or implied?

The story is about opening up a bank account. Think about whether the main idea is stated clearly or not. The main idea was explicit. The idea of the passage is clearly stated in the third sentence.

Example 3

The bank opened at 9:00 A.M. that morning, and I was the first one through the front door. I carried my large briefcase up to the counter and handed the clerk a slip. She smiled and then led me to one of the back offices. I waited there for about ten minutes, when the bank manager came in and shook my hand. "I'm Mr. Peterson," he said. "We spoke over the phone about the job."

Why is the person at the bank? Is the idea explicit or implied?

In the passage above, the reader is not told why the main character is at the bank. Looking at the explicit ideas and other clues, we can draw the conclusion that the main character is at the bank for a job interview.

Explicit	Implied
• The main character is excited and anxious to get inside the bank. • The main character hands the bank clerk a slip, and she leads him to a back office. • He waits there for ten minutes to see the bank manager. • Mr. Peterson is the bank manager's name, and he shakes the main character's hand.	• The main character is at the bank to interview for a job.

DISCUSS Why is it important to know about explicit and implied ideas?

Try These

1. **What is the main idea of this paragraph? The skunk is an odd animal. It lives in deserts, forests, and mountains. Most skunks are the size of a housecat, with black and white fur. The white fur is in a "V" shape.**

    Ⓐ The skunk has a white "V" shape.

    Ⓑ It is an odd animal.

    Ⓒ What the skunk looks like and where it lives

    Ⓓ Animals in the deserts, forests, and mountains

    What idea does each sentence suggest?

2. **The puppy began barking loudly. The boy was home from school. What is the implied idea?**

    Ⓐ Puppies makes a lot of noise.

    Ⓑ The boy always comes straight home after school.

    Ⓒ The boy is tired from school.

    Ⓓ The puppy is excited about the boy coming home.

    Think about why the dog is barking.

3. **What is the explicit idea in the following sentences? Jasmine was nervous about walking into the classroom. Everyone stared as she walked to her desk. This was her first day at this school.**

    Ⓐ Jasmine is a new student.

    Ⓑ Jasmine does not like school.

    Ⓒ Students stare at people.

    Ⓓ The teacher is very nice.

     Write your answer on a separate sheet of paper. Write your answer in complete sentences. Use the Extended Response Reading Rubric on page 81 to help you write your answer.

4. **Write three explicit main idea sentences about getting ready to go to the library. Then, rewrite the sentences so that the main ideas are implied. Use information from the lesson and your own ideas to support your answer.**

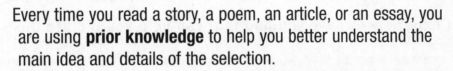

Lesson
12 Using Prior Knowledge

GETTING the IDEA

Every time you read a story, a poem, an article, or an essay, you are using **prior knowledge** to help you better understand the main idea and details of the selection.

In other words, you use information that you have learned before to make sense of what you read. This information may come from your friends, family, classmates, teachers, television, books, and more.

Let's look at an example. Read the following sentence:

Kevin looked at the snow-covered mountain in front of him.

What do I know about mountains?

What do I know about snow?

What do I know about winter?

Most likely, you can picture this scene, whether or not you have ever been on a mountain or seen snow. You can recall what you have learned from science class to help you picture the mountain. If you have ever watched a movie set in winter, you can picture how a snow-covered mountain might look.

Using prior knowledge helps you connect your reading to your own life. As you read, recall details from movies, articles, or books. Think about things you have learned in school and experiences you have had. When you consider this information as you read, your job as a reader becomes easier.

Example 1

Turkey's spice market was full of busy shoppers. The fragrance of cinnamon mixed with the smell of fresh fish. Rows and rows of brightly painted pots decorated many stalls.

What experiences have you had that can help you picture this scene?

Busy shoppers are seen on city streets, in crowded malls, and in stores. You may know the fragrance of cinnamon if you've had cinnamon rolls or toast. The smell of fish may be familiar to you if you have ever eaten seafood or been in the seafood section of the supermarket. Pots are easy to picture. You have seen them in books and kitchens. Think about what they would look like with splashes of color on them.

Example 2

Read the following sentence.

Under the water, the ocean was full of every color of fish possible, plus patches of coral and tall seagrass moving back and forth with the tide.

What experiences have you had that can help you picture this scene?

Even though you may not live near an ocean, you can use what you know about oceans to help you understand the passage. Think about what you pictured in your mind while you were reading the sentence. How many of these things do you recognize?

To picture this, you needed to know:

- What is an ocean?
- What do fish look like?
- What is coral?
- What is sea grass?
- What is the tide?
- What does it look like underwater?

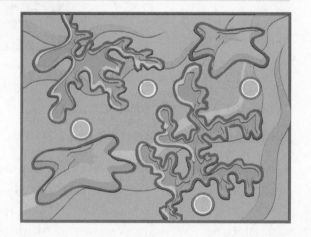

When reading a passage, it is important to organize the information that you already know to help you better grasp the passage's message.

Example 3

Read the following passage.

The airplane began to speed up as it went down the runway, and the power of the engine pushed me back into my seat. I felt a little nervous, but I had confidence in the pilot. As the plane lifted off the ground, I looked down at the land below. I saw city lights, cars, buildings, and trees. The world looked so small from up above. I wondered if this is what it felt like to be a cloud. After a little while, the pilot warned the passengers that we were about ready to land. Everyone put their seatbelts on and put their seats in an upright position. When the plane hit the ground, it was a little bumpy. The pilot put on the brakes and lifted the windbreakers on the wings. Soon, we slowed to a stop. My first flight was over, and I was excited to fly again.

Look at the questions below. Connect experiences from your own life to answer the questions. This is how you use prior knowledge to better understand text.

- What is an airplane?
- What is a runway?
- What details from the passage can I pick out from the passage that I am already familiar with?
- What details from the passage am I unfamiliar with?

NOTICE: Photocopying any part of this book is prohibited by law.

89

DISCUSS What experiences have you had that might help you understand an article about camping?

Try These

1. "The clerk was moving as fast as she could, but she still had a long line of grumpy customers." Which of the following would not be something you need to know to understand this situation?

   (A). What a clerk is

   (B) What customers are

   (C) What the customers are buying

   (D) What being grumpy is like

   Think about what is most important to know about the situation.

2. What is prior knowledge?

   (A) Information you will learn next year

   (B) Information you have learned earlier

   (C) Information that is not important

   (D) Information that is stated in past tense

   Think about what the word prior means.

3. Where does prior knowledge come from?

   (A) Teachers

   (B) Friends

   (C) Books

   (D) All of the above

4. "The camera was out of film already." Using your prior knowledge about cameras, which of the following is the best solution to the problem?

   (A) Throw the camera away.

   (B) Buy a new camera.

   (C) Put new film in the camera.

   (D) Take new pictures using the old film.

Lesson

13 Making Predictions

Have you ever solved a mystery in a book or movie before you got to the end? If you have, then you were making predictions. Most likely, you put together big or little clues, combined them with what you already knew, and figured out the ending before it happened.

For example, read this paragraph.

Joe slowly pulled on his swimsuit. Grabbing a towel, he took his place at the end of the line. One by one the other students dived into the school's pool. Finally, it was his turn. He had been worrying about this day for the last month, and everyone in his class knew it. Joe walked to the end of the diving board, took a deep breath, and looked at his classmates one last time. He knew that he would feel relieved and proud when it was all over.

What prediction can you make based on what you have read? Do you think that Joe made the dive?

Clues	Make a Prediction
• Joe is nervous about diving. • The phrase "one last time" is important. • Joe knows that he will feel good after the dive.	• Joe will make a very good dive in front of all his classmates. He will feel good that it's over.

The last sentence is the biggest clue. Joe knew that he would feel good after the dive was over. Another big clue in the paragraph is when Joe looks at his classmates "one last time." Joe will overcome his fear and make the dive.

Pay Attention to Clues

Read the paragraph below. What predictions can you make?

The sky began to get darker. There was rumble of thunder in the distance. The wind started blowing harder. Emily knew it would not be long now.

What does Emily know? Then look at the clues you have been given. What do they all seem to be leading to? If you predicted that Emily knew a thunderstorm was on the way, you are right. The dark sky, the thunder, and the wind were all clues.

Here is another example.

Everyone hid behind the couch. Susan turned the lights off and whispered, "She's almost here." Mary smiled. She knew that this was going to be great fun, and Kelly would be completely surprised.

What do you think is about to happen?

Can you predict what is going to happen next?

Clues	Make a Prediction
• Lights off • People hiding and whispering • Mary ready for fun • Kelly would be surprised	Mary, Susan, and others have planned a surprise party for Kelly.

Did you guess that there was going to be a surprise party for Kelly? If so, you are correct.

Reading All The Details

Paying attention to clues as you read can help you make predictions. Read the following paragraph. Can you predict what is going to happen? Is more than one prediction possible?

> *The car began to go faster and faster. The driver looked in his mirrors and made sure no one was catching up to him. He had worked too hard and too long to lose now. Taking a deep breath, he stomped on the gas pedal. He felt the car speed up and knew it would all be over soon.*

Think about the clues you are given in this story: There is a driver and he is going fast because he does not want anyone to catch up with him.

Did you predict that he is a bank robber? Or did you predict that he is a racecar driver? Many times the predictions you make while reading are good guesses and your predictions are correct. Sometimes, however, those guesses can be wrong. A story can take an unexpected turn. Sometimes our predictions are based on very little information. As you read deeper into the story, you get more information. These new details could change the predictions you made earlier.

Think back to the paragraph above. Here are three more predictions that could be made about this story.

1. The driver will be chased by other cars. They could be police cars or other racecars.
2. The driver will be caught by the police.
3. The driver will win the race.

Any of the above predictions might turn out to be true. It is important to review the predictions you make at different points in your reading. This will make you a more active reader. It will also help you remember details from the story better.

Before Reading	During Reading	After Reading
• Look at titles and pictures before you read. • Make predictions based on these clues.	Review predictions. Ask yourself: • Has anything happened to change your earlier predictions? • What new predictions can you make based on this new information?	Review predictions from beginning to end. Ask yourself: • How did your predictions change from start to finish? • Why did your predictions change?

DISCUSS   What clues can you use that help you make predictions before you read?

Try These

1. **What prediction can you make from this paragraph? "A mother duck and her six ducklings walked up to the curb. Each car on the road came to a stop."**

    Ⓐ The ducks will fly over the road.

    Ⓑ The cars are all in a big hurry.

    Ⓒ The ducks are crossing the street.

    Ⓓ The road is under construction.

    Why do cars usually stop for animals?

2. **What kinds of predictions can you make after reading the title of a passage?**

    Ⓐ You can predict how the story or passage will end.

    Ⓑ You can predict what the story will be about.

    Ⓒ You can predict who some of the characters will be.

    Ⓓ All of the above

3. **The little boy blew out the candles. It was finally time for cake. What is the best prediction you can make?**

    Ⓐ Dinner just ended.

    Ⓑ It is the boy's birthday.

    Ⓒ The boy was hungry.

    Ⓓ The cake was chocolate.

    Think about on what occassions people blow out candles.

4. **"The woman put on the long, beautiful dress. It looked even better than she had hoped it would. She looked in the mirror. The big day was finally here!" Which of the following events is most likely to happen?**

    Ⓐ The woman will get married.

    Ⓑ The woman will go to sleep.

    Ⓒ The woman will go to a funeral.

    Ⓓ The woman will go play soccer.

Lesson 14
Make Comparisons Across Reading Passages

GETTING the IDEA

There are many different types of reading passages. Each type provides information about a topic in a different way. For example, if you would like to know more about soccer, you could read a book about the rules of soccer and a story about a famous soccer player. If you wanted to know more about a certain movie, you could read a movie review or read a short summary of the movie's plot and characters.

Although both sources of information share the same topic, each source was written for a different purpose. By comparing what you learned in each passage, you will understand the topic even better than before.

When comparing passages, it is important to pay attention to the details. Look for ways that the passages are similar. Then, identify ways that the passages are different. When stories are being compared, study the characters, settings, plots, and themes to find similarities and differences.

When making comparisons, it is important to organize the similarities and differences that you find. **Venn diagrams** can show information that is shared between two passages, as well as what makes each passage unique.

Look at the Venn diagram below:

Movie Review
- Writer's opinion
- Likes and dislikes
- Comparison to other movies

Both
Helps moviegoer decide whether to go see a movie.

Movie Summary
- Summary of plot and characters
- Release date

Coached Reading

DIRECTIONS: Read the following passage and the poem that follows it. Look for ways that both passages are alike. Then look for ways that they are different.

FROM CATERPILLAR TO BUTTERFLY

Have you ever spotted a colorful butterfly darting from one flower to another? Have you had one land on your hand or windowsill? Butterflies are quite beautiful. Long before they become creatures with wings, however, they are caterpillars.

> Look at the title of both the passage and the poem. Is the subject the same? What clues do the titles give about the content of each passage?

They start their lives as eggs. When they hatch, they are very hungry. They begin eating. First, they eat the eggshell they came out of. Then, they start chewing on the closest leaf. It is not long until they have eaten enough that their skin no longer fits. It is far too small!

Slowly, the skin splits. The caterpillars wriggle free. They already have a new skin waiting underneath. They may be bigger, but they are still hungry. They start eating again. They chew through many leaves. It is not long before the new skin is too little again. Caterpillars change their skin a total of three times.

When caterpillars are fully grown, they find a twig. They hang upside down from it. Once again, their skin splits. This time it covers them like a warm sleeping bag. The outside turns hard. This becomes the cocoon.

> Compare the information in paragraph 4 to the information in the 2nd, 3rd, and 4th stanzas in the poem. Which provides more information, the passage or the poem?

For weeks or sometimes months, the cocoon is quiet and still. Finally, one day it splits open. The butterflies' head and legs come out first. They do not look very pretty yet. Their wings are crumpled and flat. After a while, they are able to pump blood into their wings. They start to unfold. The bright colors are seen for the first time.

Butterflies cannot fly until their new wings dry and stiffen. As soon as they are ready, the new creatures spread their wings.

BORN TO CHANGE

Born hungry,
You eat your first home.
You keep munching
And changing your clothes
To make more room.

How is the style of the poem
different from the style of
the passage?

You grow and eat,
Eat and grow,
Until the time comes
When you stop getting bigger
And go upside down instead.

In an old pattern,
You split one more time,
Covering up in a blanket
And beginning to change
From long to lovely.

Time goes on—
A quiet time—
Until a special day
When you come out
As something new.

Look at the choice of words.
What makes the selections
similar? What makes them
different?

Wet and waiting
For flight to come,
You soar to the sky
To live a short life—
A matter of days.

Flying to back yards,
Visiting briefly
Pretty flowers,
And then laying eggs
To begin again.

What new information do
you learn from the poem?

DISCUSS What differences might there be in reading a friend's letter about a vacation spot and reading a travel book about the same location?

Try These

1. **What is the main topic of both the poem and the passage?**

   Ⓐ Insects

   Ⓑ Butterflies

   Ⓒ Cocoons

   Ⓓ Leaves

   Sometimes the title of a passage or poem will tell you what the main idea or topic is.

2. **The passage calls the cocoon a "warm sleeping bag." What does the poem call the cocoon?**

   Ⓐ Blanket

   Ⓑ Shell

   Ⓒ Pattern

   Ⓓ Flight

   Think of other names that can be used for a "cocoon." Read back over the poem and find the word that replaces *cocoon*.

3. **What new information does the poem have that the passage did not?**

   Ⓐ Caterpillars are hungry.

   Ⓑ Butterflies change their skin three times.

   Ⓒ Caterpillars eat their eggs.

   Ⓓ Butterflies live a short time.

 Write your answer on a separate sheet of paper. Write your answer in complete sentences. Use the Extended Response Reading Rubric on page 81 to help you write your answer.

4. **After reading "From Caterpillar to Butterfly" and "Born to Change," which selection do you think would help you more when writing a report? Explain why. Use information from the lesson and your own ideas to support your answer.**

Lesson 15
How Graphics Help You Understand Text

GETTING the IDEA

Have you ever noticed that the titles of magazine articles or the titles of chapters in a book are printed in **bold** letters? Have you seen words or phrases printed in *italics*? Have you ever wondered why the author did that?

Authors use this strategy to make important ideas or words stand out. Words or phrases typed in bold print or italics grab the reader's attention. Teachers and writers also know that graphics can help you to better understand some of the most important or most difficult parts of a story. When you see **bold** or *italics*, you should know that these words or phrases are important to learn and to remember.

Graphic	Purpose
Bold print, font size, colored print and *italics*	Shows important words, terms, names, and places
Captions	Gives information about illustrations or photographs
Labels	Points out important information in the text or illustrations
Headings and subheadings	Identify the main idea of a paragraph or section in a reading passage

Coached Reading

DIRECTIONS: Read these two passages. Pay special attention to the graphics.

Jack Myers, Ph.D., wrote an article called "Fast Elephants." Dr. Myers describes one doctor's journey to Thailand to study the movement of elephants. Look for the different ways Dr. Myers uses bold print, italics, headings, subheadings, and captions.

WHEN ELEPHANTS GO FAST

by Jack Myers, Ph.D

For a long time, people have noticed that there seems to be something strange about the walking-to-running change in elephants. As Dr. Hutchinson wrote, "The fastest gait used by elephants has been commonly described as a walk, amble, trot, pace, rack, or running walk."

Dr. Hutchinson's partners on the team were all scientists who study *biomechanics*—how animals use their muscles to move. You can see why this team would want to study this special case of elephant movement.

This picture shows an elephant at a casual pace.

> Headings and subheadings are usually in bold print. These titles are sometimes larger than the rest of the text in a passage. The heading gives you clues as to what the story is going to be about.

> Look at the caption. What does it identify?

A Big Race

Asian elephants of Thailand were easy to study because they have been domesticated to work in fields and forests. Each elephant works with a *mahout*. A *mahout* is a man who has been with the elephant for a very long time. The mahout and the elephant communicate with each other and trust each other.

> Look at this subheading. How is it different from the heading?

> There are two words in the passage that are shown in *italics*. The definition of each one comes right after the word. Readers pay more attention to words in *italics*.

DIRECTIONS: Read the second passage. Think about what special features it includes.

THE PHASES OF THE MOON

From the earth, we can see the moon because sunlight reflects off its surface. As the moon goes around the earth, we see different amounts of its lit side. The amount of the moon we see is called its phase.

Moon Phases

When the moon is **new**, we see no moon at all. Soon after, we see the **crescent moon**, with just a sliver showing. Next comes the **first quarter**. When the moon is nearly full, with just a sliver of the side not seen, it is called **gibbous**. Then, when we see the whole side, the moon if **full**.

> What words are in **bold print**? Why are these particular words **boldfaced**?

Waxing and Waning

As the moon grows larger, it waxes, and as it grows smaller, it wanes. A waning moon goes through the same phases as a waxing moon. A complete cycle of waxing and waning happens about once every twenty-eight days.

> Take a look at these subheadings. Subheadings help the author to break up large chunks of information.

| Full Moon | Waning Gibbous Moon | Last Quarter Moon | Waning Crescent Moon | New Moon | Waxing Crescent Moon | First Quarter Moon | Waxing Gibbous Moon |

—The Phases of the Moon—

> What does the caption identify?

DISCUSS How do the special features of the article help you to understand the information?

Try These

1. **Why do writers break up their stories into smaller parts?**

   Ⓐ To organize information and make the story more understandable

   Ⓑ They need to change the subject so they put a break in the story.

   Ⓒ It gives them a reason to use short, bold titles.

   Ⓓ It makes the story look longer and takes up more space.

   Think about the material beneath headings and subheadings.

2. **What are the two subheadings from "The Phases of the Moon?"**

   Ⓐ "The Phases of the Moon" and "Waxing and Waning"

   Ⓑ "New" and "Full"

   Ⓒ "Moon Phases" and "Waxing and Waning"

   Ⓓ "First Quarter" and "Gibbous"

   Subheadings are usually larger and boldfaced.

3. **Why did the author choose to put some words in bold print?**

   Ⓐ To show excitement.

   Ⓑ They make the different moon phases stand out on the page.

   Ⓒ The reader knows these words.

   Ⓓ These words are more important than other words.

4. **"Birds use their feathers for many reasons. Feathers help them fly. They can also keep them warm when it is cold." What would be the best title for this section of a report?**

   Ⓐ Birds of the World

   Ⓑ Bird Feathers

   Ⓒ Where Birds Live

   Ⓓ Losing a Feather

Lesson

16 Using Graphic Organizers

 GETTING the IDEA
When you look through one of your math or science books, you might notice that a lot of information is in the form of charts, graphs, or diagrams. The writers do this to help you understand the information better.

Kinds of Graphic Organizers

Graphic Organizer	Purpose
Diagram 	Shows parts of something Shows how to do something Shows how something works
Table	Organizes information so it is easy to find Orders and classifies information
Bar Graph	Compares two things Orders and classifies information Plots numbers and statistics
Web	Shows the main idea or conclusion and supporting details

Graphic organizers are helpful tools for writers. They give a lot of information in a clear and organized way. These tools are especially helpful when writers try to describe dates, temperatures, or things that deal with numbers.

For example, if a writer was trying to describe how hot or cold it gets where she lives, she might write a paragraph like this:

> *We live in a place that stays hot most of the year. The average temperature is 74 degrees. Between the months of November and March, it may go down to 30 degrees. In between April and October, it may go as high as 104 degrees.*

However, it can be hard for readers to picture what these numbers represent. To help readers get a clearer picture of what it is being described, it might be better to present this information in a graph.

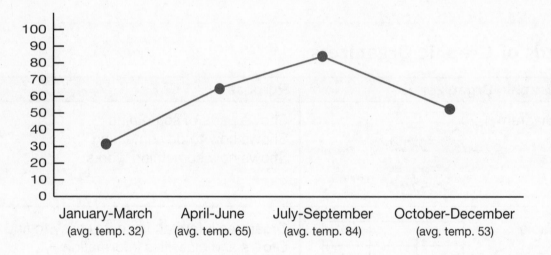

| January-March | April-June | July-September | October-December |
| (avg. temp. 32) | (avg. temp. 65) | (avg. temp. 84) | (avg. temp. 53) |

Writers aren't the only ones who use graphic organizers. Readers can use graphic organizers to organize facts and details from their reading. Read this passage about frogs and toads.

> *Frogs and toads are very similar amphibians. In fact, they look very much alike. Frogs and toads both have short bodies and are without tails. They also both make croaking sounds. However, frogs and toads are also very different. Frogs have wet, smooth skin, whereas toads have dry, warty skin. Frogs have small teeth and toads have no teeth at all. Frogs are able to jump pretty high, and toads are only able to hop short distances.*

The purpose of this article was to compare frogs and toads. A Venn diagram can help you take details from the article and compare them by similarities and differences.

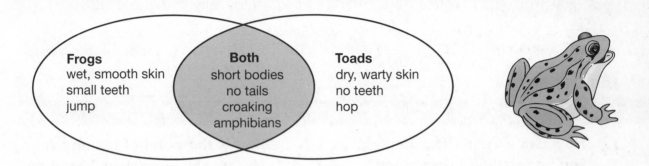

Read the paragraph below.

Mr. Reynolds took a survey to see how his fourth grade students spend their time after school. He was surprised at the number of students who watch television. He was also surprised at the number of students who play outside. He decided to show his results to the class on the bar graph below.

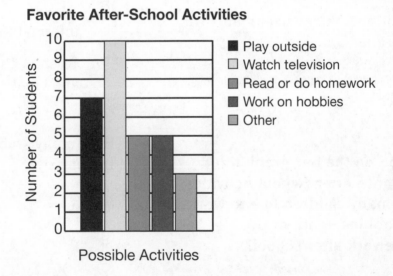

Bar graphs organize facts and numbers based on findings from reports, essays, surveys, or experiments. Plotting information on a bar graph makes the results easy to see and understand.

DISCUSS Which graphic organizer best compares the similarities between dogs and cats?

Try These

1. **How can a Venn diagram help you understand information?**

   (A) The colors make it more clear.

   (B) It clearly shows similarities and differences.

   (C) The rows and columns line up the details.

   (D) It puts things in alphabetical order.

   Think about the diagram on frogs and toads and how it shows information.

2. **Based on the bar graph titled "Favorite After-School Activities," how many children like to work on hobbies, read, or do homework after school?**

   (A) 5

   (B) 7

   (C) 8

   (D) 10

   First, figure out how many kids like to work on hobbies after school. Then figure out how many kids like to read and do homework after school. Add the number of kids that like to work on hobbies to the number of kids that like to read and do homework.

3. **What is the point of making your own graphic organizer based on what you read?**

   (A) To make the paper or report longer

   (B) To get extra credit on homework

   (C) To better understand the information

   (D) To show that you are artistic and creative

4. **How many students took part in the survey?**

   (A) 5

   (B) 30

   (C) 10

   (D) 17

Unit 2 Review

DUMBO GOES TO CAMP?

Have you ever gone away to summer camp? Did you know that some elephants in India go away to camp too? Read this informational passage about elephant camps in India.

When you think about going to camp, you might think about packing your toothbrush and bringing enough clean underwear. Perhaps you think about sitting around a campfire, roasting marshmallows and chomping on a hot dog. At a special camp in Tamil Nadu, India, there are no toothbrushes, underwear, marshmallows, or hot dogs. This special camp is for **elephants**!

The elephants of India truly deserve some time to relax. Thousands of them spend every day working different jobs. Some work at temples. They carry visitors around during festivals, weddings, and other events. Others help clear forests for logging. It is hard work.

The government realized that many of the elephants were not doing well. They were tired and having health problems. Worst of all, a few of them were becoming dangerous. They were not safe around humans. It was clear that these animals needed some time off. In spring 2003, officials set up a special elephant camp. It is located in a wildlife sanctuary. The camp is designed to give elephants a little vacation. They usually stay for a month at a time.

Camp is supposed to be fun for these elephants. A typical day includes good food, exercise, and of course, a bath. The elephants are fed a special diet of rice and lots of vitamins and minerals. They walk around the camp to get some exercise. Their favorite part of the day, however, is bathing in the river. Elephants need a great deal of water every day or they will get sick. One way they get it is through bathing.  At camp, they lie down in a river and the people scrub them clean. They play in the water and swim. Doctors are on site to make sure the elephants stay healthy.

Once elephants are well fed and rested, they return to their owners and their jobs. India's government is working hard to make sure these animals are treated well after they go back to work. With a month at camp and a little extra care, perhaps life will seem new and improved to these hard workers.

1. **Which of the following is an example of an implied idea in the passage?**

    Ⓐ Doctors are at the camp to help care for elephants.

    Ⓑ Sometimes elephants are treated badly by people.

    Ⓒ Elephants need a lot of water every single day.

    Ⓓ Most elephants stay at the camp for a month.

    1.B.1a/1.4.14   Implied Main Idea
    ---

2   **In this passage, why do you need to use prior knowledge of camps?**

    Ⓐ To understand the graphics

    Ⓑ To know if an idea is explicit or implied

    Ⓒ To understand the purpose of the elephant camp

    Ⓓ To make a comparison between Dumbo and other elephants

    1.B.1a/1.4.09   Using Prior Knowledge
    ---

3. **What prediction can you make from this passage?**

    Ⓐ India will use more and more elephants.

    Ⓑ Elephants will soon start forming their own camps.

    Ⓒ All elephants will become dangerous someday.

    Ⓓ Elephants will feel better after going to camp.

    1.B.1a; 1.C.1.a/1.4.10   Identifying Probable Outcomes
    ---

4. **Why is the word <u>elephants</u> in bold face in the first paragraph?**

    Ⓐ It is a word from another language.

    Ⓑ It is in bold print to put an emphasis on the word.

    Ⓒ It is a new vocabulary word and has a definition following it.

    Ⓓ It is a word that is not spelled correctly within the passage.

    1.B.1.c; 1.C.1e/1.4.12   Features of Informational Text
    ---

5. **If an elephant could write a letter about the camp experience, how would it be different from the descriptive passage above?**

   Ⓐ It would be very long and boring.

   Ⓑ It would be more personal and about likes and dislikes.

   Ⓒ It would make information clearer and more understandable.

   Ⓓ It would be very short and formal.

   1.C.1c; 1.C.1d/1.4.16   Make Comparisons Across
   Reading Passages

6. **Why should you use a graphic organizer when you are reading informational material?**

   Ⓐ It will make the information easier to understand.

   Ⓑ It will point out both explicit and implied ideas.

   Ⓒ It will make predictions for you.

   Ⓓ It will require prior knowledge.

   1.B.1c; 1.C.1e; 1.C.1f/1.4.11; 1.4.15   Graphic Organizers

7. **Which of the following is an example of an explicit idea in the passage?**

   Ⓐ Dumbo has visited the special camp in Tamil Nadu.

   Ⓑ Elephants need a lot of water to stay healthy.

   Ⓒ Elephants do not like to eat rice.

   Ⓓ The elephants do not like the camp because there are not any marshmallows.

   1.B.1a /1.4.14   Explicit Main Idea

 Write your answer on a separate sheet of paper. Write your answer in complete sentences. Use the Extended Response Reading Rubric on page 81 to help you write your answer.

8. **What kind of prior knowledge is important in reading this passage about the elephant camp? Use information from this unit and your own ideas to support your answer.**

Now I Can...

Use the skills checklist below to help you complete the "Now I Can . . ." statements.

Now that I know how to use _____ _____ I can connect what I already know about a topic to the text.

Now that I can use prior knowledge, I can _____ _____ about what might happen next in a story.

...Make the Connection

Place a check in the box before the skill you've mastered.

These are the skills I've learned in this unit:

☐ Explicit and Implied Idea

☐ Prior Knowledge

☐ Making Predictions

☐ Making Comparisons across Reading Passages

☐ How Graphics Help You

☐ Using Graphic Organizers

Unit 3 Reading Comprehension

Have you ever spent time reading something difficult only to feel more confused when you are done? Reading a passage or story and not understanding what you read can be frustrating. In this unit, you will learn about the many skills you can use to understand what you are reading.

Figuring out the **main idea** is important. Once you know it, you will have a better idea of what kind of information will follow. As you read, you will find that authors provide you with **major** (essential or important) details and **minor** (less important) details. All of these details support the main idea of the story.

One way to make sure you understand something you just read is to **summarize** it. Could you explain the main idea in just a few sentences? Could you write a short paragraph that includes the most important details? If you can, then you are doing a great job in comprehending, or understanding what you read.

Being able to draw a conclusion about what you are writing can help you as well. You can do this by combining your **inferences** with **prior knowledge**. You could also get a great deal of information from graphics, such as diagrams or charts.

Recognizing whether a statement is a **fact** or an **opinion** is also important. Knowing the **author's purpose** in writing is also helpful. Authors write to persuade, entertain, and inform. It is important to be able to tell the difference.

Try This

Separate into teams of five. You will need five copies of the local newspaper.

- Student 1: Read one of the lead news stories from the cover of the newspaper. Write down your conclusions about the article.
- Student 2: Find a chart, diagram, graph, or map in the newspaper and write down what conclusions you can draw from looking at it.
- Student 3: Read one of the letters in the editorial section and write down how many facts and how many opinions you found in it.
- Student 4: Find something in the newspaper that lists instructions. Write down whether they were complete enough for you to understand or if important ideas were missing.
- Student 5: Find one advertisement and write down how the author persuaded you. Find another article an author wrote to inform. How do they differ?

Lesson 17

Making Inferences

GETTING the IDEA

Suppose your teacher is handing back your tests from last week. As she walks by you, she puts the test face down on your desk and smiles. "Nice work," she says. Before you look at your actual test grade, you can probably guess that you did well on your test based on your teacher's actions. This is called **making an inference**.

Authors often expect you to make inferences when reading. They give you details and expect you, as the reader, to **infer**, or guess, the meaning from it. Sometimes those inferences are clear. Sometimes it takes some extra effort to figure them out.

For example, what can you infer after reading this passage?

Ramón stretched the back of his legs again. He bent sideways in each direction to loosen up his muscles. The number he had been given was pinned to his shirt. He looked around at all of the other runners waiting in the park. They looked nervous too. After all, this was going to be a long run, and there were some great prizes for those who finished in the top ten. Ramón just hoped to reach the finish line.

What can you infer from this passage? Where is Ramón?

What is he getting ready to do? How is he feeling?

None of these questions are directly answered in the passage, but you have been given the details to figure them out. Ramón is in a park about to run a race with other people. He is nervous and worried that he might not finish the race.

By making good inferences, you can greatly increase your understanding of what you are reading. You can see the meanings that are directly stated and what the author wants you to figure out.

Coached Reading

DIRECTIONS: Read this nonfiction passage. Try to make inferences as you read.

IS LUNCH READY YET?

What is black and white and always hungry? In this case, it is one of the world's rarest mammals: the panda. Sadly, today there are only about one thousand of these animals left in the wild. Most of them can be found in the high mountains of southwestern China.

> You can infer that the panda population is in trouble. They could become extinct.

Pandas spend almost all of their waking hours eating. They nibble on a fish now and then, or even small animals. The food they crave the most, however, is bamboo shoots and leaves. Even though they love the stuff, they have to eat a lot of it to stay healthy. For the average sized panda, this means eating 275 to 330 pounds of bamboo every week! At least twelve hours a day, they hunt for more bamboo to eat. They sit up, grab it between their large paws, and start chomping. To get enough of it in them before the day ends, they have to eat it quite fast too.

One look at a piece of bamboo and you realize that pandas must have very strong teeth. In fact, their teeth are just right for grinding up this plant. They are wide and flat. They can crush the thick stuff. Pandas have strong jaw muscles too. They have to in order to spend half of their day chewing! In addition, they also have extra-tough linings in their stomachs and throats. This way they can swallow the bamboo without getting hurt.

> You can infer that pandas need bamboo in order to survive.

Even though most of their diet is made of bamboo, pandas like to eat different species of it. In the past, that was easy to do. They could move from the top of one mountain to another in search of new kinds to taste. Now the valleys that they used to cross are full of people, and the pandas have to stay in one area of the forest. Pandas are very shy. If they run out of bamboo, they are in real trouble.

DIRECTIONS: Read this fictional passage. Where can you make inferences?

adapted from THE CAVE THAT TALKED: A TALE FROM INDIA

retold by Jyoti Singh Visvanath

Long ago, deep in a forest, a jackal discovered a cave. He decided to make it his home. He left his cave every morning to hunt for food, and returned in the evening.

In the same forest lived an old lion. The old lion wandered through the forest looking for food. But as he was too old to hunt, he often had to go hungry.

One day the lion, out hunting, tripped on a branch and landed near the mouth of a cave. He picked himself up slowly and walked to the cave's entrance. There seemed to be no one there. He sniffed. Aha! His nose told him that an animal lived in this cave. Sooner or later it would return home.

The lion licked his lips. "At last I'll get something to eat," he thought. "I will hide in this cave and eat the animal that lives here as soon as it enters."

> You might infer that the lion is going to eat the animal when it returns.

Later the jackal returned to his cave. As he walked toward the entrance, he noticed something strange. Near the mouth of the cave were footprints of some big animal. He saw that the footprints went into his cave but did not come out. That meant the animal was still inside. He wondered what to do. Then he had an idea.

"Oh cave, my dear cave," he shouted. "Please talk to me." There was no reply. "Why are you so quiet?" called the jackal. "You promised to greet me every day when I came home." Still no reply. "All right! If you will not speak to me, I will go to the other cave that talks," said the jackal. He made sounds showing he was leaving.

> You might infer that talking to the cave is part of the jackal's plan to trick the lion.

The lion sat in the cave, wondering what was happening. He heard the jackal call out to the cave, but the cave did not reply. "The cave must be keeping quiet because I am here," thought the lion. "If I call out a greeting, the jackal will come into the cave, and I can eat him up."

The lion roared out a greeting. The sound bounced off the cave walls and came out through the mouth of the cave. It was loud enough for all the animals in the forest to hear.

The jackal quickly understood that a lion was hiding in his cave. Chuckling to himself, he said, "Long years through these woods I've walked, but I've never heard a cave that talked." Then he ran far from the cave to find himself a new home.

DISCUSS What inference can you make about how smart the lion is and how smart the jackal is?

Try These

1. **What inference can you make about pandas in southwestern China?**

   Ⓐ Pandas are not very smart animals.

   Ⓑ Pandas are not able to move very fast.

   Ⓒ Pandas are tired of eating bamboo.

   Ⓓ Pandas are in danger of becoming extinct.

   Think about the tone of the passage to make an inference.

2. **What inference can you make about "The Cave That Talked"?**

   Ⓐ The cave doesn't always feel like talking.

   Ⓑ The cave doesn't really talk at all.

   Ⓒ The lion interrupted the cave's speech.

   Ⓓ The jackal will never find another cave that talks.

   Think about why the cave doesn't respond.

3. **What do you need to have to make an inference?**

   Ⓐ Samples and graphs

   Ⓑ Questions and answers

   Ⓒ Details and clues

   Ⓓ Characters and settings

    Write your answer on a separate sheet of paper. Write your answer in complete sentences. Use the Extended Response Reading Rubric on page 81 to help you write your answer.

4. **"The ice glistened under the bright lights. Dozens of children were putting on their skates. The sound of shoppers was louder than the music on the speakers." What can you infer about this scene? Write a paragraph explaining your inference. Use information from the lesson and your own ideas to support your answer.**

Lesson 18

Main Idea

GETTING the IDEA

To figure out the **main idea** of what you are reading, you have to sort through details (big and small) and spot the central concept of the passage. Until you can recognize the main idea, it can be quite hard to understand what you are reading. Once you have a grasp of the main idea of any passage, you can start to focus on the details around it to learn more.

Let's look at an example. If this were the first paragraph of a story, what do you think the main idea would be?

The painter took out a blank canvas. He uncovered his paints and grabbed a clean brush. It had been more than six months since he had painted his last portrait and he could not wait to start another—even if it was going to be a picture of a man's favorite pet chicken!

Look at the information in this paragraph. It talks about a canvas, paints, brushes, and portraits. It even talks about chickens. So, what is the main idea?

The main idea is an artist is starting a portrait.

Read this paragraph:

The peacock spread its beautiful tail feathers wide. Many people stopped to look and admire them. Even the monkeys in the next cage were jumping up and down. The polar bears on the other side did not seem too excited though. It was certainly a great day to pay a visit to the city's new zoo.

Here, the main idea is a trip to the zoo. The animals in the passage are the details that make the main idea more interesting.

Coached Reading

DIRECTIONS: Read the passage. Think about the main idea and how it is supported.

HOW DOLPHINS SNOOZE

by Jack Myers, Ph.D.

Do dolphins sleep?

That's a good question. A dolphin is a mammal, not a fish. It must come to the surface to breathe. So how does it manage its breathing and sleeping?

To find out, I asked two friends to help us with an answer. The first is Greg Early. He is a specialist on marine mammals. Here is his reply. "When scientists and veterinarians first tried to anesthetize dolphins (give them drugs to make them sleep), they found that the dolphins stopped breathing as soon as they were anesthetized (They quickly learned to use a machine to keep the dolphins breathing.) This led to the thought that dolphins do not sleep the same way that you and I do. It is generally thought that dolphins take short 'catnaps' but are never completely asleep. As someone who got his start working the midnight shift at the aquarium, I can back this up myself.

"There was also a little work done on examining the brain activity of dolphins that showed that one side of a dolphin's brain was more active when it was 'sleeping.' So the common belief has been that dolphins literally sleep 'with one eye open.'"

> Many times the title of a passage will give you a clue to the main idea.

> Often, the first paragraph will give clues about what the main idea is. This one focuses on exactly the question we are wondering: "Do dolphins sleep?"

> This paragraph is loaded with supporting details. It tells how animal doctors noticed that the dolphins stopped breathing when they were anesthetized. This suggests that dolphins don't sleep through the night like humans, but take many catnaps instead! These details help support the main idea.

> Each paragraph has a main idea, too. Can you spot the main idea of this paragraph in one sentence? If you said, "Dolphins literally sleep 'with one eye open,'" you had the right idea!

I asked the second friend, Dr. Terrie Williams, who studies dolphins and has two of them as pets at her home in California. Here is her reply.

"Greg mentioned what we do know. The thought is that dolphins can sleep with one half of the brain resting while the other half remains awake. There have been observations of Pacific white-sided dolphins swimming in pods, where they keep one eye open watching their buddies while the other eye is shut during the night. In that way, half of the brain can catch up on sleep; the other half of the brain will sleep later."

> The second sentence of this paragraph shows that a new idea is coming: that dolphins rest one half of the brain at a time! The new idea will support the main idea, too.

"Our two dolphins tend to get very quiet at night, especially after eating dinner. Sometimes they will rest, floating at the surface, and other times they will find a quiet spot on the bottom of a pool to sleep. They will stay motionless underwater for minutes at a time, then float up to the surface, take a quick breath or series of breaths, and then sink back down. We tend to think of these quiet periods as 'sleep' for the dolphins. It is especially apparent because the rest of the time they are active and swimming.

> Here, we learn that dolphins have many 'quiet periods' of rest throughout the night that are their version of a good night's sleep. This detail supports the main idea that dolphins don't actually fully sleep.

"The big question is what to do in the wild when sharks or other dangers may be around. There it is probably best for dolphins to keep one eye open and travel in protective groups while they rest at least part of their bodies."

DISCUSS Why is it important to figure out the main idea in what you are reading?

Try These

1. **What would the best title be for a passage about going on a picnic?**

   Ⓐ Out to Sea

   Ⓑ A Meal in the Park

   Ⓒ A Can of Ant Spray

   Ⓓ A Game of Baseball

   Think about what going on a picnic is like. What do you do on a picnic?

2. **"The bus slowed down. George took out his ticket and picked up his bags. His long trip was about to begin." What do you think the main idea is?**

   Ⓐ Riding a bus

   Ⓑ Going on a journey

   Ⓒ Packing bags

   Ⓓ Buying a ticket

   Think about what the last sentence tells you.

3. **What do you think is the main idea of a passage titled "My Four Feathered Friends"?**

   Ⓐ Dogs

   Ⓑ Bicycles

   Ⓒ Birds

   Ⓓ Pillows

4. **How do you know you have found the main idea of a passage?**

   Ⓐ All of the action and details revolve around it.

   Ⓑ The author states the main idea in the first sentence.

   Ⓒ It is included in the very last paragraph of the story.

   Ⓓ The main character states it in a conversation.

Lesson

19 Supporting Details

GETTING the IDEA

Suppose that you are an architect. You have spent weeks creating a drawing of a new building. After many months, it is no longer a drawing, but a real building, sitting on a lot in the middle of the city. Although you came up with the idea, you did not create the building alone. You had a lot of help from construction workers, carpenters, plumbers, electricians, and many more. Together, you created something new and wonderful. It was a team effort.

When you read or write something, it is also a team effort in some ways. The main idea is the architect and the drawing. The team who helps takes the idea from paper to an actual building is the details. Look at this example:

The cake was lovely. Elaine would think it was perfect.

The main idea is clear: someone named Elaine was going to like a cake. Can you picture the cake in your mind? No? That is because the team hasn't come in to help you yet. Here are the details:

The huge cake was lovely. It had pink and red roses on the top and green leaves trailing down the sides. In the middle was a figure of a girl with a cap and gown. Elaine would think that this graduation cake was perfect.

Now can you picture this cake? The details have made it come alive. Each detail supports the main idea—a cake that Elaine was going to love.

Major and Minor Details

Sometimes details are very important; without them, the story might not make sense. For example, if you were writing a book report, you would want to include **major** details like the book's title and author. Without that information, it would be hard for the reader to understand what you are writing about. However, other details that you might include, like what year it was published, or how many pages the book has, are less important, or **minor**. If you took them out of your report, it would still make sense. While they add extra information, or flavor, to your writing, they are not necessary.

When you are reading something, stop and look at the details that support the main idea. Which ones are the most important? Which ones could be left out?

Detail Webs

One way to better understand a passage is to create a detail web. First, draw a circle and write the topic of the text in the middle. Then connect smaller circles to it. Write the supporting details in the outer circles.

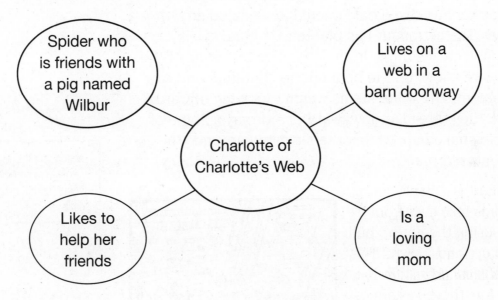

What did you learn about Charlotte after reading this web? As you learned in Lesson 16, graphic organizers are an excellent way to sort and view information from a story or text in a new way. Webs are perfect for organizing story details. They can help you remember details by making a picture of the character's traits in your mind.

Coached Reading

DIRECTIONS: Read the passage. Note what details are used to support the main idea.

FARMING IN SPACE
by Amy Hansen

What will astronauts eat when a space voyage takes years or even decades?

Lots of fresh vegetables, says Dr. Mary Musgrave of the University of Massachusetts. She has spent the last ten years learning how to grow plants in space. And it's a good thing she has already started her work, because extraterrestrial gardening can be tricky.

> Dr. Musgrave is an expert on plant growth in space. She has spent ten years learning how to grow plants in space, and she works at the University of Massachusetts. These are important details.

In 1997, while the Mir Space Station spun around Earth, astronaut Mike Foale peered at a sealed growth chamber. The astronaut has planted Dr. Musgrave's quick-growing seedlings in the chamber, but none of the stems were showing. He opened the container and saw the problem. The white stems weren't growing upward. Instead, they threaded downward or sideways. Some of the roots snaked up, while others twisted around. These were confused plants.

> Think about the details that are given to show that it is difficult to grow seeds in space.

On Earth, a plant's roots and stems take cues from gravity, using the Earth's pull to find "up" and "down." This process is called *gravitropism*. On the Mir, there was almost no gravity. Dr. Musgrave came up with a solution: give the plants more light. This idea made sense because plants also use sunlight to find their way— a process called *phototropism*.

> Which detail is used to support the idea that the seedlings needed more light?

And it worked. Once the seedlings had more light, the stems turned up and the roots went down. Now Dr. Musgrave was free to worry about the next problem. Would her baby plants live to flower?

Many plants died in space. But Dr. Musgrave thought she knew why. She thought the space plants were starving for air. Plants live by taking up carbon dioxide from the air. Since a plant uses up this gas in the air around it, the plant needs air currents to bring more carbon dioxide close to its surface.

These details explain why the space plants were starving.

On Earth, the air is always moving. Gravity pulls down cold air, and warm, lightweight air rises. So the air is shifting even when we can't feel a breeze. And with these shifts, plants get plenty of carbon dioxide.

Many earlier experiments with plants in space had used closed chambers. On the Mir Space Station, Dr. Musgrave tried a new greenhouse that had a fan pulling in a constant supply of the air inside the space station. The plants loved it. They flowered and even produced more seeds, which Mike Foale was able to plant and grow. Using Dr. Musgrave's method, he completed the first seed-to-seed experiment in space, and moved one plant closer to an extraterrestrial garden.

Details are given here to support the idea that the plants loved the additional air.

"And this," says Dr. Musgrave, "is good news for long-term space travel."

DISCUSS Why is it important to recognize the supporting details in what you are reading?

Try These

1. **What is the purpose of details in a passage?**

   Ⓐ To make the passage longer

   Ⓑ To support the main idea

   Ⓒ To confuse the reader

   Ⓓ To explain the ending

   Think about a story you know well. What do the details leading up to the plot do?

2. **If the main idea is Simon's new neighbors, which of the following is most likely a supporting detail?**

   Ⓐ It is October nineteenth.

   Ⓑ The family moving in has three children.

   Ⓒ Watching television is fun.

   Ⓓ It's time for dinner.

   Think about what is a relevant detail to a neighborhood.

3. **How do you know if a detail is a minor one?**

   Ⓐ It comes towards the end of the passage.

   Ⓑ It can be left out without affecting the story.

   Ⓒ It explains something important about the main point.

   Ⓓ It does not have any real meaning.

4. **If you are writing a book report, which of the following details would be considered major?**

   Ⓐ The number of pages

   Ⓑ The year it was published

   Ⓒ The title of the book

   Ⓓ The colors on the cover

Lesson

20 Summarizing

GETTING the IDEA

Once you have figured out the main idea and supporting details of a story or passage, you can begin to put together a summary. A good summary hits the high points and tells you what a story or passage is about. You take all that you read and shrink it down to the most important ideas and details.

Being able to write a good summary of what you read is an important skill. Often times, writing a summary will help you better comprehend a story or passage. When you write a summary, you should address the main idea and all of the major supporting details. Minor details are less important and should be left out of summaries

Let's look at an example. Suppose that you just finished an article about how tea is made in Taiwan. Look at these two examples of summaries. Which one is the best?

Summary A	Summary B
Tea is very important to the people of Taiwan. They drink it at every meal and even in between. They grow many different kinds of tea, with many flavors. The process of growing and harvesting tea leaves is quite complicated. It takes a lot of time and effort.	They have a lot of tea in Taiwan. It is grown in many different areas of the island. The people drink it at breakfast. They have it other times too. The best kind is called dingdong oolong. It tastes strange but the people seem to like it. It takes a long time to grow tea. It takes a long time to harvest it too. It is often wrapped up in special bags and crushed to bring out its flavor.

Summary A is a very short summary that gives the reader the main idea quickly. Summary B is a longer summary with too many unimportant details. These details are unnecessary for a short summary.

Coached Reading

DIRECTIONS: Read the passage. Think about what details you would include when putting together a summary.

WELCOME TO THE WORLD'S FAIR!

Karen's eyes just kept getting wider by the minute. She knew that the World's Fair was supposed to be surprising, but she had had no idea that it would be this surprising! She had never seen such incredible things in her whole life. Even though it was nighttime, the whole place was lit up like it was the middle of the afternoon, thanks to the lights powered by Edison's invention. She thought it was called electricity.

Karen had been so thrilled to find out that the 1893 fair was being held in her hometown, Chicago. When she got

back home later that night, she knew that she would talk non-stop about it all. She would tell her mother all about the displays that showed what life had been in faraway places like Egypt and India. Her dad would want to know about the Viking ship model on the water, and her younger brother would be full of questions about the wild animal show she saw.

> Which details are major? Think about which details should be included in a proper summary?

"Karen! Come on. Let's get in line," shouted Beth, her best friend.

"In line for what?" replied Karen.

"Look up, silly!"

Karen turned and gasped. She looked up, and up, and up. She had heard rumors about this in town but had thought everyone was kidding. Now that she was standing in front of it, she realized they were serious.

"How could anything be this tall?" asked Beth. "I mean, how is it possible?"

"Maybe this will tell us," said Karen, pointing to a sign to their left. The girls walked over to read it.

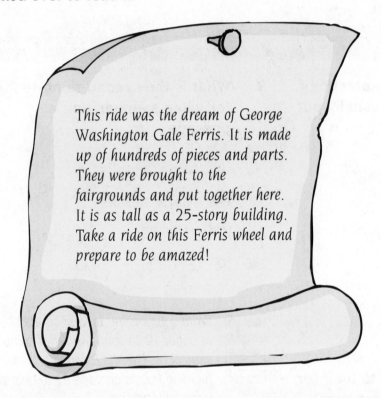

This ride was the dream of George Washington Gale Ferris. It is made up of hundreds of pieces and parts. They were brought to the fairgrounds and put together here. It is as tall as a 25-story building. Take a ride on this Ferris wheel and prepare to be amazed!

Although there are a lot of details included in this sign, only a few need to be included in the summary. Which ones are essential?

Karen looked over at the line. It was very long, but how she could miss out on a chance to ride on the Ferris wheel? It took over an hour for the girls to get their turn. With thirty-six cars, each able to hold sixty people, it did not take as long as Karen had first imagined. They spent most of the time watching the two 500-horsepower steam engines that were there to turn the huge wheel.

As Karen and Beth climbed into one of the cars, Karen did some quick math. Each ride held over 2,000 people. As the wheel began to turn, however, all thoughts of numbers flew out of her mind. When she reached the top, she could see more of the world than she had ever seen before. Way in the distance, she spotted water. It was Lake Michigan!

When the ride ended and the girls touched ground again, neither one of them could say a word. The Ferris wheel was everything it was promised to be, and they were honestly amazed! Karen could hardly wait to get home to tell her family all about it.

Think about which detail would be most important to include at the end of your summary.

DISCUSS How does being able to summarize help you understand this entire passage?

Try These

1. When you summarize something, in what order do you usually put the information?

(A) From beginning to end

(B) Minor details first

(C) Alphabetical order

(D) No order is needed

Think about how stories are told.

2. What is the first thing to look for when summarizing a passage?

(A) Minor details

(B) The main points

(C) Inferences

(D) Conclusion

If someone asked you to summarize "The Three Little Pigs" in three sentences, what part of the story would you tell them?

3. What is the second thing to look for when summarizing a passage?

(A) Minor details

(B) Major details

(C) Title

(D) Ending

 Write your answer on a separate sheet of paper. Write your answer in complete sentences. Use the Extended Response Reading Rubric on page 81 to help you write your answer.

4. Summarize "Welcome to the World's Fair!" in your own words. Use information from the lesson and your own ideas to support your answer.

Lesson 21 Sequence of Events

GETTING the IDEA

The **sequence of events** is the way a story is organized from beginning to end. The first event comes before the second event for a reason, and the second event comes before the third event for a reason. The ability to look over a story, poem, or article and point out the sequence of events is another way to help you understand what you read.

Read the following sentences.

Planting a flower garden is not difficult. First, you pick out your seeds. Then you water the ground. Next, you dig holes two inches deep and one inch apart. After that, you get a small shovel. Finally, you get to pick the flowers. Just make sure the seeds are completely covered with dirt before you begin to water the soil.

Feeling a little confused? You should be. These instructions are out of order. The sequence needs to be corrected or else planting a flower garden will be a disaster.

What would be the correct order? What is the sixth step?

As you read, take time to note the order in which events happen. If you read a story about a girl answering the phone, but the phone doesn't actually ring until much later in the story, something is wrong. Some things must happen in a certain order.

Time-order words such as *first*, *next*, and *last* can help you understand the order of events. Watch for time-order words and see how the sequence can make it easier to follow what you're reading.

1	get seeds
2	get a shovel
3	dig holes
4	cover seeds
5	water the ground
6	

Coached Reading

DIRECTIONS: Read the passage. Pay attention to the order of events in the story.

WINNING THE RACE

Field Day at Greenmont Elementary was just weeks away. This was always a fun day at school. On Field Day, students in grades one through six competed in some games that were silly and some that were serious. Samantha could not wait for field day. Last year, she had been sick and missed out on the fun. To make matters worse, Samantha's twin brother Joey won a blue ribbon in the mile run. Samantha remembered how Joey bragged about his victory.

"You should have seen me. As soon as they blew the whistle I took off. No one could catch me. I really think that I was faster than lightning!" Joey bragged.

This year would be different. Samantha was determined to beat her brother in this event. Samantha carefully prepared for the race. First she asked her mother to buy her a new pair of running shoes. Samantha was convinced that good shoes would help her to win the race. Then she began training.

> The words *first* and *then* tell you the order of events in this paragraph.

Every day after school Samantha hurried home. After a quick snack and a change of clothes, Samantha headed for the running track at the park. At the park, Samantha stretched her legs and then took off running. Her friend Tessa sat in the bleachers with a watch so that she could time how long it took Samantha to run a lap around the track. Samantha would run until her legs wouldn't move. Before leaving the park each afternoon, Tessa would let Samantha know how long it took for her to run a lap. Samantha kept a chart in her journal to show how much faster she was getting.

After only two weeks of training Samantha could feel her legs getting stronger. Samantha could tell by the chart in her journal that she was getting faster. Samantha was sure that she could win the race!

What words tell you the events in this paragraph come last?

At last Field Day had arrived. Field Day began with some silly games, such as the three-legged race and a race to roll an egg to a finish line. Samantha giggled as she watched Tessa push her egg to the finish line. Next came lunch. Samantha was nervous and couldn't finish her hot dog. Finally it was time for the mile race to begin.

Samantha took her place on the start line. Joey smirked at his sister standing next to him. Samantha just grinned and waited for the signal to start the race. When the whistle was blown, Samantha took off. She quickly passed the other runners. Samantha ran faster and faster. Samantha looked over her shoulder as she crossed the finish line. Joey gave his sister the thumbs up sign. Samantha had won the race and broken the school record.

A chart is a useful tool that can help you order the events of a story.

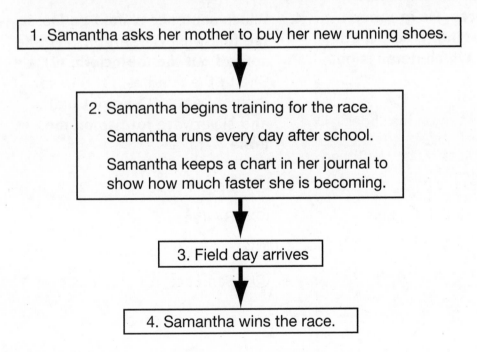

1. Samantha asks her mother to buy her new running shoes.

2. Samantha begins training for the race.

   Samantha runs every day after school.

   Samantha keeps a chart in her journal to show how much faster she is becoming.

3. Field day arrives

4. Samantha wins the race.

NOTICE: Photocopying any part of this book is prohibited by law.

131

DISCUSS Why is it important to know the sequence of events in what you are reading?

Try These

1. **What happens if events are not written in the proper order within a passage?**

   Ⓐ The reader will get confused.

   Ⓑ The story will be funny.

   Ⓒ The passage will be boring.

   Ⓓ The reader will finish sooner.

   Think about the steps you take to get dressed in the morning. What would happen if you put your sneakers on first?

2. **"Joshua slipped on his shoes. He tied the laces. He grabbed his backpack. Finally, he pulled on his socks." Which detail is out of place?**

   Ⓐ Joshua slipped on his shoes.

   Ⓑ He tied the laces.

   Ⓒ He grabbed his backpack.

   Ⓓ Finally, he pulled on his socks.

   Pretend you were Joshua. What would you do first?

3. **Which sentence should go first in the following paragraph? (1) Jake put the key in the door. (2) He turned it. (3) The lock opened and he walked into the house. (4) He pulled his keys out of his pocket.**

   Ⓐ Sentence 1

   Ⓑ Sentence 2

   Ⓒ Sentence 3

   Ⓓ Sentence 4

4. **Which sentence should go last in the following paragraph? (1) She spread out the tablecloth. (2) She lit the candles. (3) She sat down to eat. (4) She put plates and silverware for two on the table.**

   Ⓐ Sentence 1

   Ⓑ Sentence 2

   Ⓒ Sentence 3

   Ⓓ Sentence 4

Mix It Up

THE LOST LAKE

by Allen Say

> Read the second part of "The Lost Lake." Dad and the narrator are going on a camping trip to catch some fish. Dad knows a special place.

"It's a bit of a hike to the lake, son," Dad said.

"I don't mind," I told him. "Are there any fish in the lake?"

"Hope so. We'll have to catch our dinner, you know."

"You didn't bring any food?"

"Of course not. We're going to live like true outdoorsmen."

"Oh . . ."

Dad saw my face and started to laugh. He must have been joking. I didn't think we were going very far anyway, because Dad's pack was so heavy I couldn't even lift it.

Well, Dad was like a mountain goat. He went straight up the trail, whistling all the while. But I was gasping in no time. My knapsack got very heavy and I started to fall behind.

Dad stopped for me often, but he wouldn't let me take off my pack. If I did I'd be too tired to go on, he said.

It was almost suppertime when we got to the lake.

The place reminded me of the park near Dad's apartment. He wasn't whistling or humming anymore.

"Welcome to the Found Lake," he muttered from the side of his mouth.

"What's wrong, Dad?"

"Do you want to camp with all these people around us?"

"I don't mind."

"Well, I do!"

"Are we going home?"

"Of course not!"

He didn't even take off his pack. He just turned and started to walk away.

Soon the lake was far out of sight.

Then it started to rain. Dad gave me a poncho and it kept me dry, but I wondered where we were going to sleep that night. I wondered what we were going to do for dinner. I wasn't sure about camping anymore.

I was glad when Dad finally stopped and set up the tent. The rain and wind beat against it, but we were warm and cozy inside. And Dad had brought food. For dinner we had salami and dried apricots.

"I'm sorry about the lake, Dad," I said.

He shook his head. "You know something, Luke? There aren't any secret places left in the world anymore."

"What if we go very far up in the mountains? Maybe we can find our own lake."

"There are lots of lakes up here, but that one was special."

"But we've got a whole week, Dad."

"Well, why not? Maybe we'll find a lake that's not on the map."

"Sure, we will!"

We started early in the morning. When the fog cleared we saw other hikers ahead of us. Sure enough, Dad became very glum.

"We're going cross-country, partner," he said.

"Won't we get lost?"

"A wise man never leaves home without his compass."

So we went off the trail. The hills went on and on. The mountains went on and on. It was kind of lonesome. It seemed as if Dad and I were they only people left in the world.

And then we hiked into a big forest.

1. **Why does Dad laugh when his son asks if he brought any food with him?**

    Ⓐ He thinks it is silly that his son would expect him to bring food with him.

    Ⓑ He thought that his son had brought the food with him in his backpack.

    Ⓒ He brought food and is laughing at his son's shock that he might not have.

    Ⓓ He is planning on not eating while he and his son are on the camping trip.

    1.B.1a/1.4.17   Making Inferences

2. **Why was Dad upset when he found other people at Lost Lake?**

    Ⓐ He knew that all the camping spots would be taken.

    Ⓑ It was a special place to him that he didn't want to share.

    Ⓒ He was worried that his son would be bored there.

    Ⓓ It was not legal for other campers to be at this specific lake.

    1.B.1a/1.4.17   Making Inferences

3. **What is Dad's main point of taking this trip with his son?**

    Ⓐ To go fishing

    Ⓑ To get some work done

    Ⓒ To spend time together

    Ⓓ To get some exercise

    1.C.1b; 2.A.1a/1.4.17   Making Inferences

4. **Which detail best supports how Dad feels when he sees other people at the lake?**

    Ⓐ He gets out the food for dinner.

    Ⓑ He stops whistling and humming.

    Ⓒ He takes out his compass.

    Ⓓ He sets his backpack down on the ground.

    1.C.1b/1.4.13; 1.4.18   Supporting Details

5. **Which of these is the best summary of the story so far?**

Ⓐ Lost Lake has been discovered by many people over the years.

Ⓑ A father and son set out for a camping adventure with challenges.

Ⓒ Bringing extra food on a camping trip is an important step.

Ⓓ A son and his dad are looking for a place to go fishing together.

1.C.1b/1.4.20   Summarizing

6. **Which event happens first in this part of the story?**

Ⓐ The son gets tired of carrying the heavy backpack.

Ⓑ The father finds other people at Lost Lake.

Ⓒ The two of them sit down and have dinner.

Ⓓ The son worries that his dad didn't bring food.

1.C.1d; 1.B.2b/1.4.21   Order of Events

7. **Which of these words best summarizes Dad's attitude towards looking for another lake further up in the mountains?**

Ⓐ Angry

Ⓑ Thoughtful

Ⓒ Delighted

Ⓓ Confused

1.C.1b/1.4.20   Summarizing

8. **Which statement from the story best shows that Dad is prepared to hike a long way?**

Ⓐ "There are a lot of lakes up here, but that one was special."

Ⓑ "There aren't any secret places left in the world anymore."

Ⓒ "We're going cross-country, partner."

Ⓓ "We'll have to catch our dinner, you know."

1.C.1b/1.4.13; 1.4.18   Supporting Details

9. **Which of these events happens last in this portion of the story?**

(A) They see other hikers ahead of them on the trail.

(B) They decide to search for another lake further up.

(C) They start hiking through a forest.

(D) They have salami and dried apricots.

1.C.1d; 1.B.2b/1.4.21   Order of Events

Write your answer on a separate sheet of paper. Write your answer in complete sentences. Use the Extended Response Reading Rubric on page 81 to help you write your answer.

11. **Explain what details in the story help you to infer how Dad feels about Found Lake. Use information from the passage and your own ideas to support your answer.**

1.C.1b/1.4.13; 1.4.18   Main Ideas and Supporting Details

10. **What is Dad's main idea when he and his son leave Found Lake?**

(A) To head back home

(B) To buy more food

(C) To find another lake

(D) To go back to Lost Lake

1.C.1b; 2.A.1a/1.4.18; 2.4.03   Plot and Subplot

Lesson 22 — Making Inferences

GETTING the IDEA

As you probably remember from Lesson 17, making inferences means to look at what an author doesn't actually say, but instead, implies, or suggests. For you to understand that information, you have to look at the material in the passage and put it together with prior knowledge, or what you already know. Then, you make what is sometimes called an "educated guess." Here's an example:

The sign in the window said "Open" but all of the lights in the restaurant were turned off. The chairs were stacked upside down on top of the tables, and I could not see anyone inside.

What inference can you draw from this? Let's look at the stated information: an open sign in the window, no lights, chairs upside down, and no one inside. Combine that with what you know about stores and restaurants. Did you infer that perhaps someone forgot to change the sign?

Here is another example.

> *Kelly took the pizza box from the delivery man. She*
> *handed him the money and then closed the door. She*
> *carried the box over to the kitchen table and yelled,*
> *"Dinner time!" to the rest of the family. As everyone came*
> *to the table, she flipped open the box. Everyone stopped*
> *talking, and Kelly made a face.*

What can you infer from this example? Look at what you were told: Kelly ordered a pizza, she put it on the table, everyone came to eat and, when the box was opened, something happened. What was it? The author does not tell you, but you can infer something is wrong from the way everyone reacted.

Pay Attention to Clues

Read the next paragraph. What can you infer from the information provided?

> *Lisa tied the apron around her waist. It was going to be a long*
> *afternoon. She was helping out in her aunt's bakery, and they had*
> *a huge order of cookies to make for a children's birthday party the*
> *next day. Lisa had planned to spend a few hours at her friend's*
> *house, but she knew her aunt really needed the help.*

> Think about what clues this passage gave you about Lisa's plans and character. What is important to her?

The clues show you that Lisa is a kind person who wants to help her aunt out of a tough situation, even though she had other plans. You can infer something about her character that the author did not state but implied instead.

Could you infer anything else about Lisa? You could infer that Lisa is very loyal to her family. She is willing to put off what she wants to do in order to help her aunt. You could also infer that Lisa comes from a hard-working family. The order her aunt must fill is huge. Yet, she did not turn down the order because it would be a lot of work.

Do you now have a better idea of how to infer things when you read? Can you see how making an inference is a lot like making an educated guess?

Coached Reading

DIRECTIONS: Read this passage. Think about what inferences you can make as you read.

Fred loaded the tent and sleeping bags into the trunk of the car. The cooler was full of ice and food, and there were more boxes of snacks still in the house, ready to be brought out.

Fred ran through his checklist in his mind: bug spray, sunscreen, and first aid kit. He had packed all of these things in his backpack. But wait, he thought, what about his binoculars and bird guide book? He ran upstairs to the den and got both.

The fishing poles were carefully strapped to the car's roof, and Fred's backpack was on the front seat. Now all that was left was to grab the compass and map his dad had given him, and he would be ready to leave.

> Often, clues are in the details of a sentence. If you think about the objects Fred is packing, they will give you good clues to where he is going. Where do you go when you bring your tent and your sleeping bag?

> If you think about the objects Fred has packed, they will give you good clues to where he is going. Can you infer from these where he is headed?

DISCUSS Why is it important to be able to infer information while you are reading?

Try These

1. **The doctor took a close look at his patient. The problem was serious. A bandage would take care of it. He was sure the patient would be back on all fours chasing mice by afternoon. What can you infer about the doctor in this paragraph?**

   (A) He is a confused doctor.

   (B) He is a brand new doctor.

   (C) He is an animal doctor.

   (D) He is an excellent doctor.

   Look at the clues. There is nothing mentioned about the doctor's skills, and he does not appear confused. The clues are about the patient he is examining.

2. **What do you need to do when you make an inference?**

   (A) Make a prediction

   (B) Make a careful comparison

   (C) Make an educated guess

   (D) Make a conclusion

   An educated guess is another way of making an inference. You are guessing, but you are also using your own knowledge, as well as writer's clues, to do so.

3. **When you make an inference, where does a lot of the information come from?**

   (A) Prior knowledge

   (B) Other people

   (C) Contrasts

   (D) Predictions

 Write your answer on a separate sheet of paper. Write your answer in complete sentences. Use the Extended Response Reading Rubric on page 81 to help you write your answer.

4. **Explain how inferences play a part in helping you to understand what you are reading. Use information from the lesson and your own ideas to support your answer.**

Lesson

23 **Drawing Conclusions**

Now that you are an expert on making inferences, it is time to take it one step further: **drawing conclusions**. This happens when you take your inferences and combine them with the clues the writer has given you. Being able to draw a conclusion when you are reading will help you understand the ideas better.

Let's look at a few examples.

Lucas came running into the room. He could not wait to tell his parents the news. He knew that they would be so excited. They had helped him study for three days, and they knew how important it was for Lucas to get a good grade.

What conclusion can you come to about this passage? Look at the clues: Lucas was eager to share some news that would also make his parents happy. From that, you can infer that it is good news. Next, it says that he studied and that his score was important so you can infer that it has to do with a test of some kind. If you put those inferences together, you can draw a conclusion: Lucas had just done well on a test.

Have you ever heard the expression, "You are jumping to conclusions"? This simply means that you reached a conclusion without getting enough information first. For example, read the following.

> *Charlie took the paper from his teacher. He held his breath. Even though he studied, Charlie was still worried. He was so nervous that he was afraid to look at the words on the paper.*

If you came to the conclusion that Charlie was about to take a test, you might be right—but you could be wrong. There is simply not enough information here to know. Charlie may have been getting ready to take a test or maybe he was getting the graded test back from his teacher. Don't jump to conclusions too quickly.

Here is another one. This one is tricky, so pay close attention to the clues to make sure you are making the right inferences.

> *Jay was silent as he watched the rabbit. He did not make a sound. He did not want the rabbit to know he was watching from behind the tree. Carefully he looked to make sure the rabbit was in just the right place. He had planned on shooting it for days and finally, the lighting was just right. The darkness of the shadows would make the rabbit's white fur stand out even more clearly. Jay was sure it would be the perfect shot. Maybe he would even put it on his wall.*

> If you put together the fact that he was hiding and watching a rabbit from behind a tree, you can infer that he does not want the rabbit to know he is there. What did you infer about Jay? What clues did the author give you?

Before drawing a conclusion, review what you know or what you have just learned.

- Jay is silent.
- He is watching a rabbit.
- He does not want the rabbit to know he is there.
- He wants to be sure the rabbit is in the right place.
- He has planned on shooting it for some time.
- The lighting is just right.
- The darkness of the shadows makes the rabbit's white fur stand out.
- Jay is ready to take the perfect shot.
- Jay plans to put it on his wall. (Here's a clue! Do you know what "it" refers to?)

Did this lead you to the conclusion that he is a hunter?

Perhaps you are wrong. Read it again. Did you notice those clues about lighting and color? If you study them, you will see that you can infer that Jay may not be a hunter at all, but a photographer. Jay is planning to shoot a picture. He will be putting the picture he takes on his wall. Remember—you have to read the clues very carefully.

The words that an author uses certainly help you draw conclusions. Sometimes, however, those clues can come in other forms. Think about your textbooks or picture one of the magazines you like to read. Many of them will give you important information in the form of a chart, map, graph or diagram.

Let's look at an example. If you were studying a chart of the average amount of rain that fell in your city each year, what conclusion could you come to by just looking at it? From the data in the chart you could conclude which months were the wettest and which months were the driest.

What kind of conclusions can you come up with just from looking at this chart? Can you tell which month is coldest? Hottest? Can you tell if this place has four seasons? Yes, you can.

Which is the best month to go to the beach?
If you chose August, you are right. That's the hottest month!

Which is the best month to build a snowman?
If you chose January, you are right. That is the coldest month.

Month	Average Temp.
January	26
February	30
March	44
April	56
May	67
June	78
July	81
August	90
September	79
October	68
November	43
December	32

DISCUSS   Why is it important to be able to draw conclusions while you are reading?

Try These

1. **What does it mean to "jump to conclusions"?**

    Ⓐ To watch for clues in the passage

    Ⓑ To make inferences from clues

    Ⓒ To decide what has happened too soon

    Ⓓ To draw a conclusion based on a chart

    Think about the phrase. What does it mean to jump? It means getting somewhere quicker and in this case, it can mean making a mistake.

2. **What do some authors use to help you draw the correct conclusion?**

    Ⓐ Maps, graphs, and charts

    Ⓑ New vocabulary words

    Ⓒ Tricky or false clues

    Ⓓ Other passages

    Read each choice carefully. Which would an author use to increase your understanding and allow you to draw an accurate conclusion?

3. **"The teacher wrote her name on the blackboard. She picked up the attendance sheet and began calling out names to see who was there. The students wondered what she would be like."**

    What can you conclude from this paragraph?

    Ⓐ The students are not paying attention.

    Ⓑ The principal is coming.

    Ⓒ The teacher has not taught this class before.

    Ⓓ The class is getting ready to take a test.

4. **Besides clues, what do you need to think about before drawing a conclusion?**

    Ⓐ Homonyms

    Ⓑ Inferences

    Ⓒ Opinions

    Ⓓ Predictions

Lesson
24 Making Generalizations

GETTING the IDEA

Imagine that you just read a book about horses, and it was one of the best books you'd ever read. You might make a generalization that horses are fascinating. Now imagine that you read a magazine article about soccer, and it was boring. You might make a generalization that soccer is boring, too. If you see a two year old screaming in the grocery store, you might make a generalization that all two-year-old children are badly behaved. Is this true? Not necessarily.

A **generalization** is a broad statement. When you make a generalization, you find something common among many different details. You base a generalization on facts and prior knowledge.

Generalization	Supporting Facts and Details
Most teachers are women.	Two out of every ten teachers are men.

When you make a generalization, you are taking a little information and making a big inference about it. If you do it correctly, it can help you understand what you are reading. If you do it incorrectly, however, you can make a big mistake!

Example 1

Read this passage.

Cathy looked carefully at the apple. When she turned it over, she wrinkled her nose and frowned. Holding the fruit away from her body, she hurried over to the trash basket and threw the apple away.

What generalizations can you make from this?

Did you decide that Cathy had a bad apple? You are probably right. Was the apple unpleasant? Yes, it probably was. If, however, you generalized that Cathy hated apples or hated all kinds of fruit, you might be right—or wrong. The author does not give you enough clues for you to be able to make that generalization.

Example 2

What generalization can you make based on the following information?

1. *The Junior Rangers donated $200 to help hurricane victims in Florida.*

2. *Last year the Junior Rangers collected books to donate to the Children's Hospital.*

3. *The Junior Rangers cleaned up litter at the local park.*

The details above show that the Junior Rangers provide help for those in need. You might generalize that the Junior Rangers are a service organization.

Coached Reading

DIRECTIONS: Read the following examples. Think about what kind of generalizations you can make about each.

1. Liza walked down the city sidewalk. Suddenly a young man ran right into her. He was on a skateboard and was not even looking where he was going. He almost knocked her down.

> What kind of generalization can you make from this story? If you said that this young man was a bit rude, you are probably right. If you said all young men are rude—or all skateboarders are rude, that would most likely be wrong.

2. Pam listened to a new song on the radio. She liked the music and the words. She turned the volume up and started nodding her head to the beat. She wanted to remember everything about the song.

I wonder what group this is? She thought to herself. Then the disk jockey came on and said, "That's the latest song from Ham and Egg's new album, *Early in the Morning*.

Pam smiled and nodded knowingly. I knew it was them! She thought to herself.

> Could you generalize that Pam likes a lot of "Ham and Egg's" songs? Probably. Pam nodded knowingly after the disc jockey identified the group. This means she knows some of their other music. Since it was already stated that she likes the music and words, you could generalize that Pam likes a lot of "Ham and Eggs" songs.

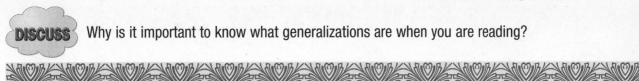

DISCUSS   Why is it important to know what generalizations are when you are reading?

Try These

1. "The library was closed. Sue was upset. She would have to wait another day before she could get the book she needed to do her homework assignment." What is the best generalization you can make from this paragraph?

   Ⓐ Libraries close too early.

   Ⓑ Sue is upset all the time.

   Ⓒ Sue will get her book tomorrow.

   Ⓓ Homework is always hard to do.

   Look at the clues given in these statements. What can you safely assume or generalize about the situation?
   ---

2. Why do you have to be careful when making generalizations?

   Ⓐ They can be wrong.

   Ⓑ They are hard to make.

   Ⓒ They are confusing.

   Ⓓ They are boring.

   If you do not know enough information or do not wait until you have all the details you need, you can make an incorrect generalization.
   ---

3. "The Civil War movie was fascinating. Julie loved the costumes and scenery. She wanted to know more about that period in history." What is the best generalization you can make from the these sentences?

   Ⓐ The Civil War is fascinating.

   Ⓑ Julie really liked this movie.

   Ⓒ Historical costumes are pretty.

   Ⓓ Julie loves to study history.

4. "The train pulled into the station fifteen minutes late. The rain was pouring down. People began to run back inside the depot." What is the best generalization you can make from these sentences?

   Ⓐ Trains are often late.

   Ⓑ It rains harder at train depots.

   Ⓒ People like to be out in the rain.

   Ⓓ Some people do not want to get wet.

Lesson 25 Fact and Opinion

GETTING the IDEA

Do you know the difference between a fact and opinion? Sometimes they can be confusing. A **fact** is something that can be proven. It has proof, which can be found in references such as encyclopedias or textbooks. An **opinion**, on the other hand, is just what someone thinks or feels about a subject. Authors use both facts and opinions in their writing. Being able to recognize whether something is a fact or opinion will help you understand your reading. You will know what to trust as truth and what to recognize as someone's thoughts or feelings about a subject.

Let's look at an example. Look at the two passages below. They are both about the same topic: Steven Spielberg.

Steven Spielberg was born in 1947. He made his first big movie in 1975. The name of the movie was "Jaws" and it was a hit. It was only the first of them, however. He also directed "Close Encounters of the Third Kind," "E.T.," "Jurassic Park," and three "Indiana Jones" movies.	Steven Spielberg was born in 1947. He is the best director on the planet. He has made the most important movies in history, including "E.T." and "Jurassic Park." His movies make millions of dollars and will do so for years and years to come.

While these two passages are about the same topic, one is based on facts or things that can be proven. The other one is made up mostly of opinions.

Example 1

Look at the chart below.

fact	opinion	statement
X		1. Steven Spielberg was born in 1947.
X		2. He made his first big movie in 1975.
		3. His first big movie was "Jaws."
	X	4. He has made the most important movies in history
X		5. His movies make millions of dollars.
		6. His movies will make millions of dollars for years and years.

What are statements 3 and 6?

If you said that 3 was a fact, you are correct. This is a fact that can be looked up in an encyclopedia. If you said that 6 was an opinion, you are correct. There is no way of knowing for sure that all of Steven Spielberg's movies will make money for years and years.

Example 2

Let's look at some more examples. Look at the statements below. Write an "F" in the blank for fact and an "O" for opinion.

___ 1.   That actor is the best looking man in the whole world.

___ 2.   Paper was first invented in China.

___ 3.   Blonde haired people have more fun.

___ 4.   Men are smarter than women.

___ 5.   All high school graduates should go to college.

___ 6.   Water boils at 212 degrees F.

___ 7.   There are three feet in one yard.

___ 8.   Swimming is the most fun sport.

Coached Reading

DIRECTIONS: Determine whether each sentence is a fact or an opinion.

Where the Wild Things Are is one of the best children's books ever written.

> The adjective *best* and the word *ever* are commonly used to express opinions.

Where the Wild Things Are was written by Maurice Sendak in 1964.

> By adding the name of the author and the date the book was written the opinion became a fact.

The *Peanuts* cartoon was created by a man named Charles Schulz.

> Can this statement be proven?

The *Peanuts* cartoon is the funniest one ever published in a newspaper.

> Think about whether this statement can be proven or not. Watch out for words like *best*, *always*, and *never*. These words are clues that an opinion is coming.

Why is it important to know the difference between fact and opinion when you are reading?

Try These

1. **How can you tell if a statement is a fact?**

    Ⓐ It will say so.

    Ⓑ Writers only use facts.

    Ⓒ It can be proven.

    Ⓓ Facts have numbers.

    Not all facts are numerical, nor are they clearly stated.

2. **Which of the following is an example of an opinion?**

    Ⓐ Computers are the best invention of the last 100 years.

    Ⓑ Computers are used in many different kinds of work today.

    Ⓒ Computers need some sort of power in order to operate.

    Ⓓ Computers are able to hold a great deal of information.

3. **Which of the following is an example of a fact?**

    Ⓐ Books are always better than movies.

    Ⓑ Pilots have the best job in the world.

    Ⓒ Football is a popular sport the United States.

    Ⓓ It always rains in Seattle and Oregon.

    Beware of sentences that include the words always or never. They are almost always a sign of an opinion. Which one of these can be proven?

4. **What is an opinion?**

    Ⓐ A statement that can be proven

    Ⓑ A feeling or belief

    Ⓒ A concluding sentence

    Ⓓ A number or date

Lesson 26 Following Instructions

Instructions are step-by-step directions that tell you how to do something. Have you ever been reading instructions on how to make something and suddenly found that you are lost? This usually means that a step was forgotten. If directions are not complete, the person reading them can easily get confused. Not only is this frustrating, but it can result in a real mess too. Imagine that you were following a recipe. The "add one cup of flour" statement was left out. Most likely, your dish would not turn out right.

It is easy to miss a step when writing out directions. If you do something every day, it becomes so familiar that you don't think about it anymore. You just take that step for granted.

Look at this set of directions for something as simple as checking out a library book:

1. Take the book to the checkout desk.
2. The clerk will scan the bar code on the book.
3. You will be given a receipt with the due date on it.
4. Keep the slip so you know when to bring the book back.

Are there any steps missing? Think about exactly what happens when you go to the library.

- You find a book you want to read.
- You take it to the checkout desk.
- You hand the clerk your library card
- The clerk scans the bar code on your card and on the book.
- The clerk stamps the due date on a piece of paper.
- You keep the piece of paper so that you know when the book must go back to the library.

In the first description, is there any mention of needing a library card? That is an important step and if it had been left out, the process would not have worked.

Consider Each Step

Let's look at another set of directions for writing and mailing a letter.

Example

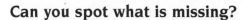

1. Get a piece of paper.
2. Write a letter to your grandparents.
3. Fold the letter.
4. Put it in an envelope.
5. Put your return address in the corner.
6. Take the letter to the post office.
7. Put it in the outgoing box.

Can you spot what is missing?

Think about what you do when you are writing and getting a letter ready to mail. Because this is such a common task, it is easy to think that everyone will know what to do. There are two very important steps missing in these directions. Did you see them? The first one comes after step four. Although you put your return address on the envelope, there was no mention of writing your grandparents' address on the envelope. The letter can not be delivered without an address on it. The other step that is missing is putting a stamp on the envelope. If either of these steps was missed, your letter would never be delivered.

When you write, make sure the directions are complete or you might miss out on important information you will need later.

Coached Reading

DIRECTIONS: Read these directions for how to make a peanut butter and jelly sandwich. There are several steps that you must follow.

1. Gather your ingredients: bread, peanut butter, jelly, knife, and plate.

2. Open the bread bag and take two slices of bread out. Close the bread bag and put the bread away.

3. Open the jar of peanut butter. Insert the knife into the peanut butter. Scoop out a generous amount of peanut butter and spread on one slice of bread. Clean the knife or get a new knife from the drawer.

4. Open the jar of jelly. Insert the knife into the jelly. Scoop out a generous amount of jelly and spread on the remaining slice of bread. Put the bread together so that the peanut butter and jelly is on the inside of the sandwich.

5. Place the sandwich on the plate. Use the knife to cut the sandwich in half.

6. Clean up any mess.

Usually directions begin by listing all of the items you will need to gather.

Directions are written in a certain order. What would happen if you did step 3 before step 2?

Were you able to complete the task?

DISCUSS Why is it important to recognize when a set of directions is complete?

Try These

1. **Why is it important to make sure that a set of directions is complete?**

   Ⓐ To make sure you have all the information you need to complete a process or task

   Ⓑ To make sure you can find the missing steps and fix them

   Ⓒ So you can write missing steps on your own

   Ⓓ To make sure you can point out an author's mistakes to your teacher

   ---

   Think about making something like a recipe or a model. If a step is missing, you will run into trouble. You have to have all the information in order to complete a task.

   ---

2. **What can unclear directions do to you as a reader?**

   Ⓐ Confuse you

   Ⓑ Entertain you

   Ⓒ Inspire you

   Ⓓ Teach you

   Unclear directions always create problems.

3. **What step is missing in the following set of instructions on how to brush your teeth?**

   1. **Turn on the water.**
   2. **Uncap the toothpaste.**
   3. **Put some on your toothbrush.**
   4. **Brush your teeth.**
   5. **Rinse and spit.**
   6. **Rinse and put away the toothbrush and toothpaste.**

   Ⓐ Go to bed.

   Ⓑ Turn off the water.

   Ⓒ Put on your pajamas.

   Ⓓ Set your alarm.

    Write your answer on a separate sheet of paper. Write your answer in complete sentences. Use the Extended Response Reading Rubric on page 81 to help you write your answer.

4. **Write the steps involved in how to sharpen a pencil. Use information from the lesson and your own ideas to support your answer.**

Lesson 27 Author's Purpose

Why do you think an author writes something? He or she has a purpose or reason behind the words. Knowing the author's purpose will help you to understand what you are reading better and will make sure you are looking at it with the right attitude. The usual purposes for a writer are to entertain, to inform, or to persuade.

For example, biographies, articles, and reference books inform or teach you something. Plays, poems, short stories, and novels are generally written to entertain you. Ads and letters to the editors are often written to persuade or to get you to do something.

Look at this statement. What do you think the author's purpose was in writing it?

> *This new laundry soap is amazing! It can cut through grease or grime that you can get on a shirt. Your laundry will be sparkling clean and all your friends will want to know your secret. Better yet, this laundry soap can be yours for only $4.99.*

If you guessed that this writer was trying to convince you to buy this soap, you are right. The author uses words like amazing and sparkling clean to help persuade you.

Example 1

Sally hopped across the room on one foot clucking like a chicken. This was the last time she would ever bet her brother she could beat him at chess.

What do you think the writer was trying to do here?

Did you guess entertain the reader? You are right. Imagining Sally hopping across the floor might make you laugh.

Example 2

Look at the statements listed below.

Persuade	Entertain	Inform	
X			1. This is the best movie ever made, and you simply have to go and see it.
		X	2. The kangaroo is an Australian animal that has a pouch in the front.
	X		3. Julie looked like a canary, but she could eat like an elephant.
		X	4. Soccer involves moving the ball across the field without using your hands.
X			5. I am definitely the perfect person for this job, and you have to hire me.
	X		6. Jackie laughed as she climbed into the tiny cockpit on the airplane.

Can you figure out which ones are meant to inform, entertain and persuade?

How could you tell what the author's purpose was in each of the statements? One way is to stop and ask yourself how you feel about what you just read.

- Do you have the feeling the author wants you to agree with him/her about something?
- Do you feel like you have just learned something or do you just feel like you enjoyed what you just read?
- Your response to the words can help you figure out what the author's purpose was in writing them.

Coached Reading

DIRECTIONS: Read these two passages. Think about what each author's purpose was for writing the text.

To the Editor

The Rockwell Cement Company should forget about their plans for the cement plant in Midville. The plans call for an enormous plant. It would be seen for miles. The plant would be an eye sore in the community. It would also be a danger to the community. The plant would create a lot of pollution. This would affect both our water and our air quality.

> The author is trying to get readers to share her point of view.

> The author makes it clear that she feels the cement plant should not be built.

Helpful Insects

Many people don't like bees. They are afraid of being stung. However, without these helpful insects, we would not have many of our favorite flowers or fruits. When bees drink nectar from flowers, they carry away pollen on their bodies. They leave the pollen on the next plant they visit. This helps the plant to reproduce.

> This author is trying to convince people that bees are helpful, harmless insects.

DISCUSS Why is it important to identify the author's purpose when you are reading?

Try These

1. **What is the author's purpose if she is hoping to get you to agree with her?**

   Ⓐ To persuade

   Ⓑ To entertain

   Ⓒ To inform

   Ⓓ To predict

   An author who is trying to get you to do something is trying to convince you. Think of television commercials, for example. While they may be entertaining, what is their real purpose?

2. **What is the author's purpose in this statement? "Mark Twain is the author of Huckleberry Finn, Tom Sawyer and A Connecticut Yankee in King Arthur's Court."**

   Ⓐ To persuade

   Ⓑ To entertain

   Ⓒ To inform

   Ⓓ To predict

   Are these statements trying to convince you to read these books? To entertain you with stories from them? Predict what will happen in them? Or give you new information?

3. **Which of the following is an example of persuasive writing?**

   Ⓐ A science-fiction novel

   Ⓑ An advertisement for shampoo

   Ⓒ A history textbook

   Ⓓ An announcement about the winner of a race

4. **What does the author hope to do when he/she writes to inform?**

   Ⓐ Make you learn something

   Ⓑ Make you laugh or cry

   Ⓒ Make you buy something

   Ⓓ Make you agree with him/her

Unit 3 Review

TAKING HIS BEST SHOTS
by Claudia Cangilla McAdam

> John Fielder is a nature photographer whose job takes him to the steepest, most beautiful peaks of the Rocky Mountains, every day.

John Fielder could have drowned on his way to work. His raft bumped over rocks and pitched through rapids on the Dolores River in southwestern Colorado. The spring runoff of melting snow from the mountains sent chilly water crashing down the river.

Fielder's rubber raft rushed toward "Snaggletooth," the largest rapid on this stretch of the Dolores. The raft smacked into a big rock in the middle of the 100-foot wide river. Thousands of pounds of water poured over the edge of the boat, securing it against the rock and drenching Fielder. He was in big trouble.

Luckily, another group of rafters came by. They set up a "Z-rig," a system of pulleys secured by a tree at the side of the river. It took seven people two hours to free Fielder so that he could continue on to work.

Who goes to work in a rubber raft? As a nature photographer, Fielder often travels to work in unusual ways. In spring, he rafts the river to reach hidden canyons. In summer, three llamas carry his equipment, and helpers trek the rugged land with him. In winter, he skis the back country, traveling five to nine miles a day to get from one remote hut or cabin to another.

During the past thirty years, Fielder has recorded half a million images with his camera. He calculates that between the driving, hiking, skiing and rafting he's done, he's logged more than a million miles in Colorado.

And Fielder does not travel light. "I want to make nature look as good as I can on film," he says. To get great shots, he lugs sixty-five pounds of equipment on his back as he hikes or skis. It takes him as much as half an hour to set up his camera for each shot. Fielder photographs with a large-format camera like those used a hundred years ago. He has to tuck his head under a black cloth to look through the view finder, which presents the image to him upside down.

"Nature photography is an art form," Fielder says. "The camera is a great tool because it does the 'painting' for us."

Fielder's adventures in the wilderness have been funny (chasing down a pack of runaway llamas). They've been uncomfortable (getting soaked by summer monsoons and pelted by golf-ball sized hailstones). They've been annoying (marmots—animals in the groundhog family—chewing through his car's spark-plug wires, stranding him three hours from anywhere). And they've been dangerous (in addition to the rafting incident, he has faced a potential avalanche, which caused him to hightail it out of the area).

"Mother Nature is powerful," Fielder says simply.

Because the natural world has given Fielder so much, he works to preserve the wild and open spaces. He treats the land with respect. In return he is able to experience the sights, sounds, and smells of different places, and share those encounters with others through his photos.

Fielder plans each trip with great care and love, and scouts out each location so that he can always take his best shots.

---

1. **Which of these can you infer from the passage?**

   Ⓐ Fielder is a brave person.

   Ⓑ Taking pictures is easy.

   Ⓒ Fielder makes a lot of money.

   Ⓓ Llamas are small animals.

   1.B.1a/1.4.17   Making Inferences

2. **In this story, the central point is that Fielder has an exciting job as a nature photographer. What is another name for the central point in a story or passage?**

   Ⓐ A supporting detail

   Ⓑ A prediction

   Ⓒ A main idea

   Ⓓ A summary

   1.C.1b; 2.A.1a/1.4.18 Main Idea and Supporting Details

3. **Which of these is a minor detail in paragraph 2?**

   Ⓐ The raft struck a rock in the large river.

   Ⓑ Water began pouring into the boat.

   Ⓒ The rapid is called Snaggletooth.

   Ⓓ Fielder was in big trouble.

1.C.1b/1.4.13; 1.4.18   Details

4. **Which of these is the best summary sentence for paragraph 6?**

   Ⓐ Fielder uses a black cloth with his large-format camera.

   Ⓑ Fielder travels often.

   Ⓒ Fielder uses a lot of heavy and old-fashioned equipment.

   Ⓓ Fielder sees images upside down.

1.4.20   Summarizing

5. **What happens first in the article?**

   Ⓐ Fielder almost drowns.

   Ⓑ The llamas carry equipment.

   Ⓒ Fielder is caught in an avalanche.

   Ⓓ Marmots chew his spark-plug wires.

1.C.1d; 1.B.2b/1.4.21   Order of Events

6. **The author implies that Fielder has had a lot of wild adventures. What must a reader do when an author only implies information instead of clearly stating it?**

   Ⓐ Make a generalization

   Ⓑ Draw a conclusion

   Ⓒ Make an inference

   Ⓓ Create a summary

1.B.1a/1.4.22 Draw Inferences, Conclusions, or Generalizations

7. **Which of these is an example of jumping to a conclusion based on the story?**

   Ⓐ Photographers lead dangerous lives.

   Ⓑ Fielder likes to go on adventures.

   Ⓒ There are some beautiful places in Colorado.

   Ⓓ Fielder respects the world of nature.

   1.B.1a/1.4.22; 1.4.24   Drawing Conclusions

8. **What can happen if you make a generalization too quickly?**

   Ⓐ You can easily be wrong.

   Ⓑ You will get confused.

   Ⓒ You will make predictions.

   Ⓓ You can make an inference.

   1.B.1a/1.4.22   Making Generalizations

9. **Which of these is an opinion in the story?**

   Ⓐ Nature photography is an art form.

   Ⓑ And Fielder does not travel light.

   Ⓒ Fielder's adventures in the wilderness have been funny.

   Ⓓ Luckily, another group of rafters came by.

   1.B.1a/1.4.23   Facts and Opinions

10. **In this story, it takes Fielder as much as a half hour to set up his camera. What happens if he misses a step in a set of instructions?**

   Ⓐ His photos may not turn out well.

   Ⓑ He will have to go back home.

   Ⓒ He will fall out his raft.

   Ⓓ His camera will be broken.

   1.B.1a/1.4.25   Following Instructions

Now I Can...

Use the skills checklist below to help you complete the "Now I Can . . ." statements.

Now that I can identify the _____ _____ _____ in a story, I can use this order of events to summarize what I have read.

Now that I can find the main idea in a passage, I can use this to guide my reading and look for _____ _____ that reinforce the main idea.

Now that I can tell the difference between _____ and _____, I can evaluate what I read and make judgments about what is true and what is merely someone's belief.

...Make the Connection

Place a check in the box indicating the skill you've mastered.

These are the skills I've learned in this unit:

☐ Inferences

☐ Main Idea

☐ Supporting Details

☐ Summarizing

☐ Sequence of Events in a Story

☐ Making Inferences

☐ Drawing Conclusions

☐ Making Generalizations

☐ Fact and Opinion

☐ Following Instructions

☐ Author's Purpose

Literary Elements and Technique

Suppose you are a tracker in the forest following the trail of a lost person. It is your job to follow the clues to figure out where the person went. As you do, you should ask yourself questions such as: Why did the person go that way? Why did she go right instead of left? What was the person like? By learning as much as you can about the person, and using all your clues, you will have a better chance of finding her.

When you read, you can also use clues to better understand a story or passage. In this unit you will pay attention to **dialog** to learn more about what a character is like. **Dialog** is the conversation, or speaking parts, from characters in a story. You will also look at a character's **actions**. What a character says and does will help you form judgments about the character.

One way to learn more about a passage is to step into the mind of the author. Think about the **setting** the author chooses. You should also think about the **plot**, or the events the author uses to make the story move forward. Recognizing all these elements when you read will help you better understand stories and passages.

Try This

Work in groups of four. Each person will need a piece of paper and a pencil.

- Work independently to complete the story below.
- Fill in the blanks using the part of speech below the blank.
- Take turns reading your version aloud.
- Identify the setting, characters, and events of the story.
- Identify ways in which the story stayed the same. Discuss how they were different.

The pilot _____ his plane. He was taking off in a few minutes and wanted to be
              verb

ready. The _____ airplane sat _____ on the runway. As soon as the _____
          adjective   adverb   noun

arrived, he would _____. Looking at his _____ map, he figured that the _____
                  verb   adjective   noun

would last about _____ hours. The pilot laughed _____. He loved flying on _____
                 adjective   adverb   noun

like this. He _____ his map and _____ put it in his pocket.
             verb   adverb

Lesson 28 Plot

Say you picked out a book at the library today. The cover looked interesting and the summary on the back of the book sounded great. You have been reading it for almost an hour and it just feels as though the story is not going anywhere.

Usually, when a book is not interesting, it means that the story did not have much of a **plot**. The plot is a series of events that makes the story go forward. A good plot helps keep your attention. A good plot makes it hard to put the book down and stop reading.

The plot of every story follows a certain format.

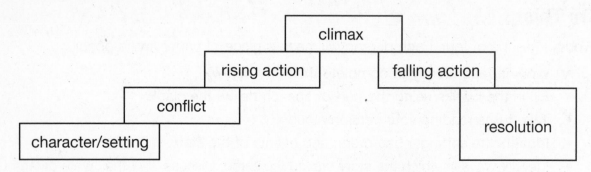

First, you are introduced to the **characters** and the **setting**.

Next, you are shown the problem or **conflict** in the story.

Third, the plot moves ahead and the **action rises** (gets more exciting).

Fourth, the story reaches its climax. The **climax** is the moment of highest excitement and is the turning point in the plot.

Then, the **falling action** occurs. In this stage, everything in the story is explained.

Finally, the story reaches its **resolution**. Here, the characters' problems are solved.

Coached Reading

DIRECTIONS: Read the following story. Notice the events that move the plot along.

THE LITTLE FLY AND THE GREAT MOOSE: A NATIVE AMERICAN STORY

retold by Janeen Adil

A very long time ago, the Merrimac River flowed peacefully through the wooded hills. Many beavers made their homes in the river, and great schools of fish lived in its pure, clean waters. So delicious was the water that thirsty animals would come to drink at the river from far and wide.

> The author has given you details about the setting in the opening paragraph. What details does she give?

Now, in this long-ago time, the largest of all the animals was Moose. Even bigger than the mighty bear, Moose stood as tall as the highest tree. When he walked, the ground shook beneath his heavy feet. And when he bellowed, birds flew before him in a panic.

> Look at the words the author uses to describe Moose. What does this tell you about his character?

One day, the giant creature learned of the Merrimac's sweet waters. I, too, will go there, Moose thought, and taste the water for myself.

> Here, the author introduces the first part of the plot.

When he reached the river, Moose immediately began to drink. The water pleased him, so he drank more and more. Soon the level of the water started to drop.

> Think about what you know about the rising action. What events make up the rising action in this paragraph?

This made the beavers very nervous. What would happen to their homes, the dams they had worked so hard to build from mud and sticks? "Help us," the beavers begged the rabbits. "We must stop Moose," they pleaded with the foxes. "Drive him away!" the beavers cried to the deer. But Moose was so big that no one—not even the bear—was brave enough to face him.

Meanwhile, Moose continued to drink from the river. The water dropped lower and lower, and now the fish were afraid. At least the beavers could move to a new home, but what would the fish do if the river dried up? And they, too, began to beg for help.

> What detail or event in this paragraph shows that the problem is getting worse?

At last, one creature volunteered to chase Moose away. It was Fly. "You are the smallest of us all!" exclaimed the animals. "How can you possibly make that huge creature leave?" And they laughed at Fly, thinking it was a fine joke.

> We are getting close to the climax of the story. What will happen next? In a well-written story, the reader will ask that question very often.

Little Fly, though, had a plan. First, she landed on one of Moose's legs and bit him. Moose simply brushed her off. Fly tried another leg, only this time she bit harder. Moose stamped his foot in annoyance. Then Fly buzzed quickly from spot to spot on Moose's brown hide, biting sharply as she went.

> The action is still rising here.

Moose was furious! He shook his immense head, snorted, stamped, and kicked. Up and down the riverbank he ran, trying to discover who was biting him. But since he couldn't see tiny Fly, Moose had no way to fight back. Finally he fled from the river as fast as he could run.

> This is the climax of the story.

How proud little Fly was! She couldn't help boasting to the animals that she had driven Moose away. "You see," Fly told them, "My size didn't matter after all. I wasn't big enough or strong enough to fight Moose. But I was smart enough!"

Moose was gone, but beside the river were prints from his massive feet. Wherever he had stamped, the earth sank, and now the Merrimac River came rushing in to fill the deep holes. No longer did the river flow quietly. Instead, it tumbled over falls and rushed noisily through rapids where Moose's feet had torn up the ground.

> This is the resolution of the story. All the loose ends are tied up.

DISCUSS Why is it important to recognize and understand the plot of a story?

Try These

1. **What is the first step in a story's plot?**

   Ⓐ Coming to a resolution

   Ⓑ Reaching the story's climax

   Ⓒ Presenting a pattern of rising action

   Ⓓ Introducing setting and characters

   Think about what you learned from the story step chart.

2. **What is the best definition of a climax?**

   Ⓐ Rising action

   Ⓑ Setting and characters

   Ⓒ Turning point

   Ⓓ Resolution

   Think about when the climax of a story occurs.

3. **What is the last step in a story's plot?**

   Ⓐ Introducing the setting

   Ⓑ Reaching a resolution

   Ⓒ Increasing the action

   Ⓓ Reaching the story's climax

4. **What is the conflict in a story?**

   Ⓐ The resolution

   Ⓑ The climax

   Ⓒ The problem

   Ⓓ The characters

Lesson
29 Theme

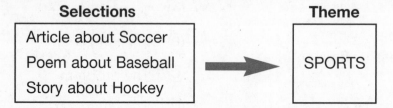

Suppose you have been invited to a party. According to the invitation, the theme of the party is Australia. When you get there, you see decorations in the shape of kangaroos and koala bears. The cake is decorated to resemble the Australian flag. Even the party favors are treats that came from the famous land "down under." This is a great example of theme. A theme is the overall main point or idea of an event or story.

Suppose that you read an article about soccer, a poem about baseball, and a story about a boy who learned how to ice skate on a hockey team. What do you think the theme of all three would be?

Selections		Theme
Article about Soccer Poem about Baseball Story about Hockey	→	SPORTS

If you read three poems—one about a telephone, one about television, and one about newspapers—what would you guess their theme is?

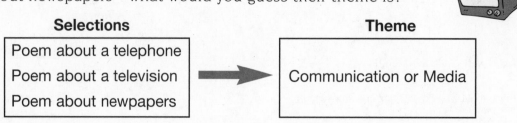

Selections		Theme
Poem about a telephone Poem about a television Poem about newpapers	→	Communication or Media

Understanding the theme of what you are reading will help you recognize common points and how details and events in a story relate to one another. The theme of a story, poem, or article is the controlling idea.

FOOTPRINTS

by Beverly McLoughland

Along the shore,
Where the sand lies
Soft and wet,
A tumbling wave
With its net of foam
Scoops up footprints
Like captured butterflies.

Will they be pinned
On some sea cave wall,
And labeled . . .

Sandpiper,
Gull,
Girl,
Boy,
Cocker spaniel pup?

Will curious little fish
Swim by to look at them?

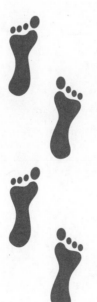

THE WAVE

by Ellen A. Kelley

First lap, it's flat as a map
folding into sky
then a giant rolling over
breathing salty sighs
next it's a water dragon's back
where fish and swimmers fly
last, a rumbling
dark freight train
that splash-and-crashes by!

THINGS TO DO IF YOU ARE THE RAIN

by Bobbi Katz

Be gentle.
Hide the edges of buildings.
Plip, plop in puddles.
Tap, tap, tap against the rooftops.
Sing your very own song!

Make the grass green.
Make the world smell special.
Race away on a gray cloud.
Sign your name with a rainbow.

Example 1

What do the three poems have in common?

Ⓐ They are about waves.

Ⓑ They are about water.

Ⓒ They are about rain

Ⓓ They are about fish.

Look at the poems carefully. *Footprints* tells the reader about how the waves wash away footprints. *The Wave* is all about the different shapes a wave of water can make. It can be flat, a giant, a water dragon, even a freight train! *Things to Do If You are the Rain* tells us about a gentle rain that makes grass green, makes the world smell good, and forms a rainbow. All three poems are about water and its presence on the Earth.

Example 2

Look at the list of subjects below and then figure out what the theme is for each set.

1. (1) a poem about snow
    (2) a story about someone who goes sledding
    (3) an article about dressing warmly

    Theme: _____

2. (1) a poem about cardinals nesting in a tree
    (2) an article about how birds build their nests
    (3) a how-to essay on building a birdhouse

    Theme: _____

Think about what each subject has in common.

3. (1) a story about a boy's bicycle
    (2) an article about today's trains
    (3) a poem about cars on the highway

    Theme: _____

Think about the uses of bicycles, trains, and cars. They are all means of transportation.

4. (1) a poem about growing daisies
    (2) a how-to essay on planting roses
    (3) an article on flower seeds

Theme: _____

Let's look at a few more examples, but from a different point of view.

Example 3

Here are five themes. What possible poems, stories, articles or how-to articles can you think of to support these themes? One category is done for you in each of the examples.

(1) VACATIONS
     Article: An article about the best vacation spots
     Story:
     Poem:
     How-to:

(2) SUMMER FUN
     Article:
     Story: A story about hiking through the Grand Canyon
     Poem:
     How-to:

(3) LIBRARY EVENTS
     Article:
     Story:
     Poem: A poem about all the different books and movies in a library
     How-to:

(4) MUSEUMS
     Article:
     Story:
     Poem:
     How-to: A guide on how to tour a museum

(5) THE PACIFIC NORTHWEST
     Article:
     Story: A story about a man's journey to California during the gold strike
     Poem:
     How-to:

DISCUSS What are common themes in many stories?

Try These

1. **What is another term that means theme?**

- Ⓐ Conflict
- Ⓑ Main idea
- Ⓒ Setting
- Ⓓ Rising action

The theme of a story is the biggest point.

2. **If you read a poem about a party, a story about a parade, and an article about a festival, what would the theme be?**

- Ⓐ Celebrations
- Ⓑ Journeys
- Ⓒ Movies
- Ⓓ Parades

Birthdays would belong with this same theme.

3. **Which of these would belong in a unit with a "dessert" theme?**

- Ⓐ Parties
- Ⓑ Ice cream
- Ⓒ Movies
- Ⓓ Sand

 Write your answer on a separate sheet of paper. Write your answer in complete sentences. Use the Extended Response Reading Rubric on page 81 to help you write your answer.

4. **Choose one theme from the list below. Write a paragraph that focuses on the theme you have chosen. Use information from the lesson and your own ideas to support your answer.**

1. Sports   4. Movies
2. Music   5. Nature
3. Books

Lesson
30 Character and Setting

GETTING the IDEA

The **setting** is where and when a story takes place. Typically there is more than one setting in a story. Each setting is important for the story plot and characters.

The **characters** are the people in the story who are part of the story plot. Characters make things happen. Characters fit into the setting that they are in. For example, you would most likely not see an Eskimo in a desert.

On Tuesday morning, Charlie went to school. He studied two subjects in the morning. First, he worked on some math problems with his friend, Carol. Then he spent a couple of hours reading and writing with his tutor, Ms. Jacoby. Finally, at the end of the school day, he learned the rules for tennis in his gym class.

When he went home from school, Charlie delivered papers in his neighborhood. This usually took about an hour and a half. He always looked forward to going to Mr. Reynolds' house. Mr. Reynolds always thanked him kindly and gave him a snack.

At the end of the day, he went home to eat dinner with his family. They had spaghetti, which was his favorite. His mother asked him how his day was, and Charlie just smiled. "It was really busy," he answered.

There are three different settings in this story and five different characters. Can you match up the characters with the setting they appear in?

Characters	Settings
Charlie	School
Carol	
Ms. Jacoby	Charlie's neighborhood
Mr. Reynolds	
Charlie's mother	Charlie's home

Charlie appears in each setting in the story. The other characters each appear in one scene. Each character appears at the place and time where they fit best.

The time period of a story is part of the setting. Read this sentence:

She pulled out the pocket computer she always carried. By plugging in the information she already knew about her location, she knew it would tell her how far away she was from the meeting point.

How would this passage be different if it took place in the year 1850?

1. The woman would not be carrying a pocket computer.
2. She would most likely have to rely on directions to the meeting point from a friend.

Coached Reading

DIRECTIONS: Read the following story. Look at the setting. Think how it affects the passage and your thoughts about the characters.

THE OLD MEN, THE YOUNG MEN, AND THE MONKEYS

by William Groeneweg

On the Caribbean island of Monserrat, people tell a story about a place they call Monkey Island. Monkey Island was small, and its people were poor but happy. What they couldn't make or grow for themselves, they bought from passing ships.

> Think about how people fit into this setting.

One of the ships that stopped there was carrying monkeys for a zoo. Some of them escaped, and soon the island was full of monkeys. They stole food, broke things, raided gardens, and teased dogs. Before long, the monkeys had become a big problem.

> Can you guess what time period this story takes place in?

One day, everyone on the island gathered for a meeting to decide what to do. They talked and talked, and finally they decided to catch the monkeys and send them to the zoo. The young men of the island, who'd all been sitting together, stood up and said that they'd catch the monkeys, for no one else was as strong or as fast as they were.

> The young men are very proud characters. They are confident in their abilities.

They chased the monkeys, but the monkeys were faster. They climbed trees to catch the monkeys, but the monkeys climbed higher. They made traps, but the monkeys were so clever that they would spring the traps and scamper up the trees, laughing.

The village elders watched and laughed, and while they watched, they worked. They made heavy clay pots with long, narrow necks, and the old women cooked delicious-smelling rice. The old men filled their pots with the rice and took them into the forest and then went back to the village for a rest. All the while, the young men and the monkeys watched with interest.

> The elders are very patient and experienced characters.

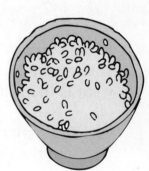

Soon the monkeys came up and reached into the pots to grab the delicious rice. Were they ever surprised! They couldn't get their paws out unless they let go of the rice, and they certainly weren't going to let go of such wonderful food!

The young men were amazed at what they saw, but they asked each other, "How will the monkeys get their paws out of the pots?"

While they were wondering, the old men came back with a bunch of bananas in a big cage. When they set the cage down, the monkeys let go of the rice and ran to get the bananas. Then the old men locked them in.

The young men were sad because they hadn't helped catch the monkeys at all, but one of the old men said, "How will we get the monkeys to the ship? This cage is too heavy to carry."

"We can carry it" said the young men and so they did.

What do you learn about the characters in this part of the story?

1. You learn that the young men are not very clever. They can't figure out how the monkeys will get their paws out of the pots.

2. You learn that the elders have a clever plan. They use bananas to capture the monkeys in the cages.

3. You learn that the monkeys are not very smart and easily fall for the elders' tricks.

4. You learn that the village elders want the young men to feel useful. The young men carry the cages to the ship, and they feel good about themselves.

DISCUSS What kinds of characters and objects would you expect to see in a story about the desert?

Try These

1. **In the story, "The Old Men, the Young Men, and the Monkeys," what is the setting?**

    Ⓐ The setting is on an island in the year 1750.

    Ⓑ The setting is on an island in the Caribbean where only monkeys live.

    Ⓒ The setting is on the island in the Caribbean called Monkey Island where people and monkeys live.

    Ⓓ There is no setting for this story.

    Think about who lives on the island.

2. **How many settings can a story have?**

    Ⓐ Only one

    Ⓑ Two

    Ⓒ Three

    Ⓓ Many

    Think about how stories can change.

3. **Which is an important element that makes up a story's setting?**

    Ⓐ Theme

    Ⓑ Time

    Ⓒ Plot

    Ⓓ Character

4. **Why do stories have to include a setting?**

    Ⓐ Without a setting, you cannot have characters.

    Ⓑ Settings help you understand where the story is happening.

    Ⓒ Without a setting, the story would be too short.

    Ⓓ Settings help the author know when the end is coming.

Lesson 31
Main and Supporting Characters

GETTING the IDEA

In books, movies, and stories, there are main characters and supporting characters. The **main characters** are the people that the story truly centers around. The main characters get the most attention in a story, while the supporting characters get less attention and are more in the background. However, supporting characters are still very important to a story. They help move the story along and interact with the main characters.

Main characters have large roles in a story. The reader gets a glimpse into their thoughts and feelings. Main characters are always part of the conflict. The problems in a story usually affect the main characters the most.

Supporting characters serve very useful roles in a story because they help move the plot along. Often times, supporting characters assist the main characters. They are the best friends, neighbors, cousins, and others who have a definite role. Often their actions affect or influence the main characters. Stories would be much less entertaining without supporting characters.

Read this example.

Timothy had been thinking for a long time about which animal would be a good pet. He always loved animals. He thought they made life so much fun.

"Hi Timothy," Tina said as she came out of the house. She was holding a small kitten in her arms. "Want to pet Sparky?" she asked. "Mrs. Robbins' cat had kittens last month. She has a lot of cats on her farm. She said I could have Sparky. He's a great pet!"

"Sure," replied Timothy. Timothy kneeled down to pet Sparky. As he began to pet Sparky's tiny head, the kitten looked up at him in delight. "He is a very handsome cat," said Timothy.

In the story, Timothy is the main character. We know his thoughts and feelings.

Tina is not a major character. Still, look at how her character helps move the plot along. She has gotten a kitten from Mrs. Robbins. She is helping Timothy decide which animal will be the perfect pet.

Coached Reading

DIRECTIONS: Read the following passage. Note how each character is described and decide which character is the main and which is the supporting character.

WHAT DO YOU DO WHEN A QUEEN COMES TO VISIT?

by Mary Houlgate

If a queen showed up on your doorstep one day, what would you expect? Would she make all your dreams come true, like in a fairy tale? Well, maybe—or maybe she'd turn your life upside down. In real life, hosting royalty can be a headache.

One of the biggest royal headaches of all times lived four hundred years ago in England. Her name was Queen Elizabeth I, and she loved to travel and stay at other people's houses— she actually slept in 241 different homes!

> The author lets you know that Queen Elizabeth I will be the main character.

Of course, Elizabeth only visited important people who owned huge houses. When she traveled, she brought more than two thousand horses and four hundred carts to carry her clothes, her favorite drinks, and even her own bed. Lots of friends came with her too. All those people (and horses) needed a comfortable place to sleep and plenty to eat. Being her host was like housing a whole parade.

> So far, the story has been all about Elizabeth. This is another clue that she is the main character.

Elizabeth was smart and full of fun. She liked poetry, music, dancing, funny plays, delicious feasts, and exciting sports like hunting and jousting. She loved expensive presents and glamorous jewelry. But best of all, Elizabeth loved praise. She never got tired of hearing how beautiful, clever, and good she was.

In 1575, Elizabeth visited Robert Dudley for nineteen days. Dudley lived in Kenilworth Castle, which Elizabeth had given him, and he wanted the queen's visit to be perfect. He built a new block of big, comfortable rooms. He planted beautiful gardens, with fountains full of fish and cages full of brilliant songbirds. He ordered cartloads of meat, hundreds of fish, and plenty of wine and beer. His cooks prepared all sorts of birds for the feasts, larks, pigeons, herons, ducklings, quails, and pheasants. One banquet had three hundred different dishes! Dudley planned dancing, hunting, plays, and dazzling fireworks, some of which even exploded underwater. And he brought dozens of expensive gifts.

> Here the author introduces a supporting character.

> Dudley helps to move the plot along by hosting the queen at his castle. He does everything he can think of to please the queen.

But on top of all this, Dudley performed a little magic. These days, we all see movies crammed with special effects, from flying spaceships to scary dinosaurs. Four hundred years ago, people also loved special effects. Dudley used them to show the queen how important she was.

When she arrived at Kenilworth, Elizabeth saw giant men blowing giant trumpets! Dudley stood his trumpeters on tall stilts covered with flowing robes. He made fake golden trumpets five feet long to cover real trumpets. Then a tree came to life! (Really, it was a man covered with moss and ivy, who suddenly jumped out of the forest and told the queen how wonderful she was.) Music came out of a giant dolphin! Dudley made a boat that looked like a dolphin. Six musicians hid inside it, and one man, a good singer, rode on top. As soon as he saw Queen Elizabeth standing on a bridge, he rode his dolphin boat over to her, singing her praises while the hidden musicians played their instruments. The queen was very flattered and amused.

What did Elizabeth do after such a wonderful visit? Dudley hoped she would thank him by making him rich and powerful. He may even have hoped that the queen would marry him. But Queen Elizabeth never married, and although Dudley continued to serve Elizabeth as an advisor and general, he died a poor man. Queen Elizabeth expected a lot, and she did not always say thank you. Maybe it's just as well queens don't come knocking on your door.

> In this final paragraph, you learn more about Queen Elizabeth's character, as well as Dudley's character.

Think about Queen Elizabeth and Dudley. Look at this list. What could you add to describe their characters?

Queen Elizabeth	Robert Dudley
Likes to travel	Likes the queen
Likes to visit people	Wants her visit to be perfect
Brings lots of friends along	Knows about what food she likes
Loves parties	Plans very carefully
Enjoys sports	Serves the queen faithfully
Very thankless and arrogant	Performs thankless tasks for queen

DISCUSS Why does it help to know which characters are main and which ones are supporting characters within a story?

Try These

1. **What is one way to know if a character is a supporting one?**

   Ⓐ He/she is not given a full name.

   Ⓑ Less information is known about these characters.

   Ⓒ Supporting characters are not interesting.

   Ⓓ These characters are only in the beginning of the story.

   Think about the stories you have read in this lesson and how you knew if characters were supporting ones.

2. **Why does an author include supporting characters in a story?**

   Ⓐ To make the story much longer

   Ⓑ To pay attention to the main characters

   Ⓒ To bring humor to the story

   Ⓓ To support the main characters

   Think about the stories you have read in this lesson and why the supporting characters are important.

3. **How can you recognize a major, or main, character in a story?**

   Ⓐ The story focuses on him/her.

   Ⓑ The author will introduce him/her first.

   Ⓒ The character announces the fact.

   Ⓓ The supporting characters all like him/her.

    Write your answer on a separate sheet of paper. Write your answer in complete sentences. Use the Extended Response Reading Rubric on page 81 to help you write your answer.

4. **Think of your favorite movie or book. Who is your favorite supporting character in it and why? Use information from the lesson and your own ideas to support your answer.**

Lesson 32

Rising Action

One of the most important parts of a good story is **rising action**. This is the part in a story where things start getting exciting. It is the part of a movie where you lean forward in your seat. It is the part where you really starting wondering, "What is going to happen next?" You have already met the characters and been introduced to the setting. You know what the conflict or problem is. Now, the action begins to rise.

For example:

- The bad guy is creeping up on the good guy.
- The ships in the space battle have fired their first shots.
- The girl has just learned that her best friend is not telling the truth.
- The horse is just about to leap over the highest fence.
- The mountain climber has just dropped her best axe and is hanging on with one hand.

Things get more difficult for the main characters. More conflicts (or problems) arise. Suspense starts to build. Characters come up with a plan and try to solve the conflict. The story plot takes on a faster pace.

Without rising action, stories would not be nearly as exciting. The rising action is what leads you to the *climax*, or turning point, of a story.

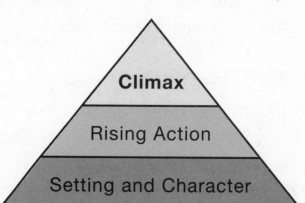

Climax

Rising Action

Setting and Character

Coached Reading

DIRECTIONS: Read the following story. Watch for signs of rising action.

THE MYSTERY OF THE MISSING SPECTACLES

by Leone Castell Anderson

"Oh my!" said Mr. Fuddle. "I can't find my spectacles." He groped about the room, looking for them. "Finders, keepers; losers, weepers," he added sadly.

> The first two characters are introduced immediately. Most likely, these characters will be the main characters. The first conflict has also arisen.

Miz Cricket gave a little leap. Mr. Fuddle was her friend. She always listened to what he had to say. She knew that he wouldn't be able to read without his spectacles, and he loved to read.

She watched as Mr. Fuddle crawled about on his hands and knees. He peered into the potted fern. He peered under the umbrella stand.

"Two heads are better than one," she thought. That was what Mr. Fuddle would say. She leaped behind him, helping him look for the missing spectacles.

The postman knocked at the door.

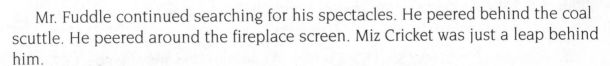

"Ah," said Mr. Fuddle, getting to his feet. "Perhaps he found my spectacles." But the postman had nothing but mail for Mr. Fuddle.

"Oh my, without my spectacles, how am I to read it?" said Mr. Fuddle. He tossed the letters onto the hall table. "Well, no news is good news," he said, and Miz Cricket nodded.

Mr. Fuddle continued searching for his spectacles. He peered behind the coal scuttle. He peered around the fireplace screen. Miz Cricket was just a leap behind him.

Then a neighbor, Mrs. McGillicuddy, knocked at the back door. "Yoo-hoo," she called. "I have something for you"

"Oh good, perhaps she found my spectacles," said Mr. Fuddle. But his neighbor had brought a plate of crumpets, his favorite treat. Mr. Fuddle invited her to share them with him, along with tea and honey. Miz Cricket sat beneath the kitchen table, waiting for the crumbs she knew he would save for her.

Just then there was a commotion at the door. It was Mrs. McGillicuddy's young son, Jeremiah. He wanted to come in.

"Perhaps he found my spectacles," said Mr. Fuddle.

But as soon as Mr. Fuddle let him in, Jeremiah spied Miz Cricket.

"A cricket!" he cried, scrambling under the table after her.

Miz Cricket leaped, just barely escaping him. "A miss is as good as a mile, as Mr. Fuddle would say," she said, panting.

> These paragraphs show the rising action of the story. The problem has gotten worse for Mr. Fuddle. His spectacles are still missing and Miz Cricket is being chased.

But "Oh my!" is what Mr. Fuddle said as he followed Jeremiah.

And "Oh thumpnoodle!" is what Mrs. McGillicuddy said as she followed Mr. Fuddle.

Miz Cricket leaped. Jeremiah jumped. Around the room they all went, leaping and jumping. Then Miz Cricket gave one last mighty leap and slid down between the cushions on Mr. Fuddle's chair.

"Enough!" said Mrs. McGillicuddy, and she marched young Jeremiah out the door.

Miz Cricket felt something hard and smooth beneath her feet.

"It's safe to come out now," said Mr. Fuddle. But Miz Cricket waited.

> These last few paragraphs are the climax of the story. The turning point is when Miz Cricket finds Mr. Fuddle's spectacles.

"Where are you?" he asked as he reached between the cushions. "Oh my!" he said. He pulled out his spectacles, with Miz Cricket clinging to them. He put them on. Miz Cricket gave a happy leap.

"You solved the mystery," said Mr. Fuddle. "You found my missing spectacles. One good turn deserves another, they say."

And Miz Cricket and Mr. Fuddle shared crumpets and tea at the kitchen table.

DISCUSS Why are the supporting characters important to the rising action within the story, "The Mystery of the Missing Spectacles?"

Try These

1. What step has to come before the rising action?

Ⓐ Conflict

Ⓑ Resolution

Ⓒ Climax

Ⓓ Plot

Think about when the first problem of the story arises.

2. What do you have to know before the rising action makes sense?

Ⓐ The resolution

Ⓑ The falling action

Ⓒ The characters

Ⓓ The author

Think about which element is most important for the author to introduce.

3. Which of the following events is part of the rising action in the story, "The Mystery of the Missing Spectacles?

Ⓐ Miz Cricket watches as Mr. Fuddle crawls on his knees.

Ⓑ The postman has mail for Mr. Fuddle.

Ⓒ Miz Cricket and Mr. Fuddle share crumpets and tea.

Ⓓ Jeremiah chases Miz Cricket.

4. What step signals that the rising action has ended?

Ⓐ The setting

Ⓑ The characters

Ⓒ The climax

Ⓓ The plot

Lesson
33 **Climax**

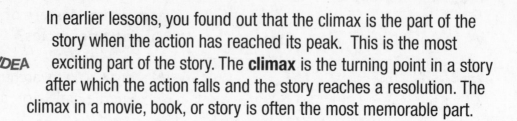

In earlier lessons, you found out that the climax is the part of the story when the action has reached its peak. This is the most exciting part of the story. The **climax** is the turning point in a story after which the action falls and the story reaches a resolution. The climax in a movie, book, or story is often the most memorable part.

The climax is often where the author will use the most exciting vocabulary words. For example, look at the two passages below.

 # 1 The music began to get louder. The song was reaching the most important part. All the musicians were concentrating on playing well. They hit the last note and the audience began to applaud.

 # 2 The music began to get louder. The notes seemed to bounce back and forth from one wall to another. The trumpets and clarinets blared and the drums pounded. The shrill tones of the flutes could barely be heard. The bows flew over the strings of the violins and cellos. The conductor's arms seemed to fly as he led the orchestra to the ending. The audience leapt to its feet as the last note faded away, and the hall thundered with the sound of delighted applause.

You should notice that passage #2 is very exciting and detailed, and therefore, is a great climax for the story. Both passages describe the same event, but passage #2 is much more memorable than passage #1.

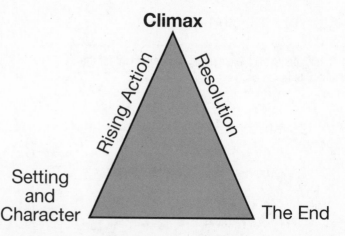

Example 1

Read the following passages. As you read, think about what makes a weak climax versus a strong climax.

> Notice how the author orders the events. The author uses vivid verbs—such as *squealed, fought, sprinted, pounding, flown*—and adjectives to help you experience the excitement of the race.

1 The red car suddenly pulled ahead by a few inches. The flag was thrown down on the track showing that this was the very last lap of the race. The driver of the blue car knew that he had to make a move. It was now or never! He took a deep breath and pushed the gas pedal down hard as he rounded the last curve. His tires squealed, and he fought to keep control of the wheel. As his car sprinted ahead of the red car, he knew he had won by less than two seconds. His pulse was pounding so hard that it felt like he had flown across the finish line.

> Without the colorful details, the passage loses some of the excitement.

2 The red car pulled ahead by a few inches. The flag was thrown on the track for the last lap. The driver of the blue car knew he had better hurry. He took a breath and pushed the gas pedal down. As the car crossed the finish line, he knew he had won by less than two seconds.

Which passage is more entertaining? Passage #1 certainly has much more detail and is much more descriptive than passage #2. Passage #1 makes you feel more involved in the action. Passage # 2 gives you a summary of the action, but fails to be thrilling for the reader.

Look at the words and phases the author uses in passage #1 to make it more exciting.

- suddenly pulled ahead
- thrown down
- make a move
- now or never
- deep breath
- rounded the last curve
- tires squealed
- fought to keep control of the wheel
- sprinted ahead
- pulse was pounding so hard
- flown across the finish line

Read passage #1 again, and pay attention to when the words and phrases in the above list pop up. These words and phrases are missing from most of passage #2.

Example 2

Now it's your turn. Read the following passage and then rewrite it to make it more exciting. Add details and change some of the verbs and nouns to make the passage better. Remember that you are writing the climax for this story. The climax is the most important part of the action.

It was finally time for the winning name to be pulled out of the hat. Suzy had been waiting a long time for this moment. She watched as the manager put his hand in the plastic bucket. There were a lot of names in there. Suzy really wanted to win the prize. She needed a bike. Finally, the manager chose a piece of paper. He pulled it out and read the name. Suzy had won!

> Recall a time when you hoped and wished for something. Did you feel nervous? Good writing causes a reader to react or respond emotionally. Recalling experiences from your past can help you connect with the feelings and emotions the writer is trying to communicate.

Before you start making any changes to this paragraph, think about the answers to these questions. They may help spark some ideas.

- How long had Suzy been waiting?
- Why did she want the bike so much?
- How did Suzy feel as he was about to read the name?
- How did the manager read out the name?
- How did Suzy react when she heard her name?
- What did the bucket look like?
- Who else was there?

Put yourself in Suzy's shoes for a moment. How would you be feeling in this situation? Use those reactions, as well as the responses to the questions above, to help you write a better, stronger climax. Write your answer on a separate piece of paper.

Why do some climaxes surprise readers?

Try These

1. **At what point in the story does the climax usually occur?**

   Ⓐ Right before the setting

   Ⓑ In the last paragraph

   Ⓒ Right after the resolution

   Ⓓ Following the rising action

   The climax is at the top of the story pyramid.

2. **Why does a story require some kind of climax?**

   Ⓐ It is a necessary part of character and setting.

   Ⓑ It is necessary for there to be a good resolution.

   Ⓒ It gives details about the story's characters.

   Ⓓ It is necessary to create the rising action.

   The climax is the turning point. The falling action follows the climax.

3. **What do authors use most when writing a climax?**

   Ⓐ Key information about where the story takes place

   Ⓑ Descriptive vocabulary words and phrases

   Ⓒ A description of the story's conflict

   Ⓓ Review of a character's traits and behaviors

4. **Which word best describes the climax of a story?**

   Ⓐ Calm

   Ⓑ Exciting

   Ⓒ Confusing

   Ⓓ Angry

Lesson 34 How Authors Portray Their Characters

GETTING the IDEA

When you read a story, you get to know different characters. It is the author's responsibility to introduce you to different characters and help you to know each character's various traits. Authors have two ways of giving the reader information about a character: they can tell you about the character or they can show that character in action.

To create memorable characters, an author has to do several things.

Authors do more than just tell you what a character looks like. They tell you how he speaks, moves, and behaves. When an author puts all of this together, he or she creates strong, interesting characters.

Cory was a young boy. He had just celebrated his 8th birthday. He was tall for his age, and so people often thought he was older than he really was. He had long, blonde hair that tended to get in his eyes and bother him when he was playing video games. His blue eyes were the color of a spring morning, and he had a laugh that made other people smile when they heard it. He had a gap between his middle teeth that made it hard for him to whistle. He called himself "a bit of a dickens," but he rarely ever made any trouble.

In this passage, the author uses descriptive words. He or she tells you important details about Cory's personality to help you get to know him.

NOTICE: Photocopying any part of this book is prohibited by law.

Coached Reading

DIRECTIONS: Read the following story. Note how the author explains a lot of the character through what she says and does.

SOMETIMES, ON MONDAY MORNINGS

by Chuck Trapkus

Sometimes, on Monday mornings, Maxine Frances Carpenter is a carpenter. Not everyone knows about it. But the woman at Doolie's Grocery Store often says, "Let's see . . . I don't remember your first name, but anyone can see you're a Carpenter."

So Maxine hauls all the wood she can carry up to her room and opens her tool closet. Her bed is really just a couple of sawhorses. Maxine measures and saws and hammers until the foreman calls out, "Coffee break!" Then Maxine joins the rest of the builders.

"Wait a minute," she says. "I don't drink coffee. I'm just little Maxine, see?"

"I don't care how little you are," snaps the foreman, "but lately you've been as quiet as a mouse."

Which is true, because Maxine is in fact a mouse, sometimes, on Tuesday afternoons. She skitters across the dining room floor searching for crumbs. She often stays in the little hole in the wall behind the sofa.

She is a very pretty mouse, with soft brown fur and long silver whiskers. But when her mother spots her crossing the kitchen counter, she screams, "AAAAAAHH! Get that awful beast!"

Awful beast? No, no—that's on Wednesdays. Sometimes. And Maxine can be quite beastly. Her hair grows until it covers most of her. Blue horns sprout from her head, and her teeth and fingernails become long and sharp.

> How is the author already showing you what Maxine's character is like? Maxine seems to be more than one character. Is she really?

She grows until she fills the room and has to squeeze through the door to get outside. "RRROAR!" she roars. She picks up a bus that is driving by. People scream.

Someone shouts, "It's from outer space!"

"No, I'm not!" Maxine roars back. "Don't be silly. I'm only Maxine. I won't hurt anyone." She puts the bus down and starts shrinking back to size. "But you are partly right," she says, "because tomorrow's the day for outer space."

> Maxine is no longer a beast, but a young girl. Why do you think that is?

Sometimes, you see, on Thursdays, Maxine is an astronaut. She usually doesn't tell her family or her friends about it, because they'd probably want to come along. She blasts off and sails through the darkness of space past planets, stars and comets. She waves at other spaceships. She floats around weightless until the radio crackles.

"This is mission control," a scratchy voice says. "Maxine, we've got a problem. You don't have enough fuel to get back. I'm afraid you're marooned."

Just in time, Maxine thinks. Because usually, on Fridays, Maxine is maroon. Occasionally she's violet, and every now and then she's bright green, but usually she's maroon. From head to toe. Even her eyes. Sometimes she can get through the entire day with no one noticing. When she sits in the maroon chair, nobody can see her at all. Until someone sits on her.

"OW!" she yelps. "It's me! Maxine!"

"So it is," her father replies. "And how's my sweet potato today?"

> Maxine's father makes her change from maroon to a sweet potato. What does this say about Maxine's imagination?

Maxine doesn't know what to say. After all, sweet potatoes can't talk. She shrinks down and shrivels up until by Saturday, sometimes, she really is a sweet potato. She rolls around the house, bumping down the stairs and hiding under the beds. And when she smells supper being cooked, she stays away from the kitchen—just in case her mother gets any ideas of making a sweet-potato side dish. Maxine just rolls around and plays quiet sweet-potato games. Before long, her mother recognizes her and says something like, "Maxine, there you are. You're being such an angel!"

And Maxine knows it must be Sunday.

DISCUSS What do you know about Maxine as a character? Why does she constantly change into something different?

Try These

1. **Which of the following tells how the author describes Maxine's character?**

   Ⓐ The author tells Maxine's story so the reader can be the judge about her character.

   Ⓑ The author explains to the reader that Maxine has a wonderful imagination.

   Ⓒ The author is lazy and doesn't tell us anything about Maxine's character.

   Ⓓ The author explains what Maxine looks like, but not how she feels and thinks.

   The author shows Maxine in action.

2. **Which of these best describes Maxine?**

   Ⓐ She is a good astronaut.

   Ⓑ She likes sweet potatoes.

   Ⓒ She has a great imagination.

   Ⓓ She is shy and likes to hide.

   Think about what makes Maxine a special character.

3. **How would you describe Maxine's mother and father?**

   Ⓐ They are annoyed by Maxine's behavior

   Ⓑ They are fun and playful with Maxine.

   Ⓒ They are angry and rude.

   Ⓓ They are sad that Maxine changes into different characters.

    Write your answer on a separate sheet of paper. Write your answer in complete sentences. Use the Extended Response Reading Rubric on page 81 to help you write your answer.

4. **Write a paragraph that describes Maxine's character in detail. Tell what kind of person she is, how she looks, and what her favorite hobbies are. Use information from the lesson and your own ideas to support your answer.**

Lesson 35
Characters' Traits: Speech and Actions

GETTING the IDEA

One of the best ways that authors can create characters in their stories is through the character's speech and actions. For example, actors in movies do this all the time. When they change roles, they take on the speaking habits and gestures of the character they are playing.

Authors will often show a lot of about a character through his or her speech. The way the character talks may tell the reader what kind of person the character is.

Another technique writers use to create a character is to show his or her actions. Readers can tell a lot by watching characters in action.

This chart shows examples of how two characters might talk and act.

Ed's Character	Tom's Character
"We have to take steps to change how this book club works."	"I'm not sure what I think. I am not sure what to do."
"I'm not going to sit here silently while people around us are writing better books."	"I'm tired, and I'm not really into worrying about all of this."
Ed walked down the alley. He knew that he must be persistent with the library president. This deal was very important for him and the other club members.	Tom walked down the alley. He didn't really care about the book club. If the book club failed, it wasn't a big deal.

What are the main differences you see in these two characters after reading how they talk and act?

- Ed is very thoughtful and outgoing. Ed cares about the book club's success.
- Tom seems to be careless and shy. Tom does not care about the book club's success.

Coached Reading

DIRECTIONS: Read the following story. Notice how the author uses speech and actions to define the main characters.

PAY ATTENTION, DONOVAN
by Barbara Youree

Donavan was always busy. When he was supposed to get dressed, he was busy watching a black ant. It was crawling up his shoestring. He wondered how it got in his bedroom.

> The author immediately gives you a clue about what kind of person Donovan is by describing his actions.

"Don-o-vaann!" his mother called. Oh, remembered Donovan, get dressed. He helped the ant out of his shoe before putting it on.

When Donovan was supposed to eat, he was watching two squirrels out the window. They were chasing each other around a tree trunk. He wondered why they didn't fall.

"Donovan, eat your cereal." His father tapped him on the arm.

"Oh, O.K., Dad," said Donovan, picking up his spoon.

At recess time in school, Donovan was still reading a story. It was about dinosaurs. He wondered if the *Tyrannosaurus rex* would eat the other dinosaur.

> Donovan seems to daydream a lot. His attention isn't always what it is supposed to be on.

"Donovan, it's time to go outside," his teacher said.

"Oh, O.K.," said Donovan, closing his book.

> Donovan responds a lot with, "Oh, O.K." He listens well when spoken to.

Donovan liked to do things right, but he always forgot what he was supposed to be doing. He didn't mean to forget. He was just too busy to pay attention.

NOTICE: Photocopying any part of this book is prohibited by law.

199

That's why he had trouble playing tee ball. He really wanted to be a good player. But he was always too busy to try hard.

"Donovan, it's your turn to bat," said the coach.

"Oh," said Donovan, picking up his bat. He had been busy waving to his mom and dad.

> What can you tell about Donovan from what he says in his mind? Authors also reveal characters through thoughts.

Donovan hit the ball hard on his third try. He watched it zip past the pitcher and skip along the ground.

"Donovan, run!" shouted his teammates.

Oh yes, run, thought Donovan as he headed to first base.

"Out!" shouted the umpire.

Not again, thought Donovan. I always forget to run. Then I'm out.

> Donovan realizes that his mind wanders. He forgets to do the things he is supposed to do.

That was the third out. Now it was his team's turn to take the field. "Pay attention this time," said the coach, patting him on the back.

"Watch the ball," said the second baseman.

Donovan tried really hard. He watched the first batter swing. Crack! The ball sailed way above Donovan's head and over the fence. Wow, he thought, I wish I could do that.

The next batter was not so good. He swung twice at the ball and missed both times. Donovan looked up and saw two jet airplanes making a big white X in the blue sky.

> Can you predict what is going to happen when Donovan sees the jet trails in the sky?

"Donovan! Don-o-vaaaan!" everyone was shouting his name.

Plop! The ball fell right at his feet. "Throw it, throw it!" shouted the pitcher. Donovan threw the ball to the pitcher. Too bad. He was supposed to throw it to first base.

The next batter stepped up to the plate. Donovan heard his father shout, "Watch the ball, son."

Donovan would try really, really hard this time. He would pay attention and watch the ball. Maybe, just maybe, he could catch it.

But first he had to check the blue sky. The white X was puffing out and fading . . . Then, another white thing appeared: the ball! It was heading right toward Donovan. Watch the ball, he remembered. He held up his glove and took two steps forward.

Plop! The ball landed right in the center of his glove!

"Yea, Donovan!"

"Don-o-van, Don-o-van, Don-o-van!" everyone cheered. Donovan's team had won the game.

"Way to go, son!" He could hear his dad's voice over the others.

"Great play," the coach said.

On the way home, his mom said, "Why don't we stop for ice cream? What do you say, Donovan?" She repeated, "Donovan, ice cream?"

"What?" said Donovan. He was busy thinking about that ball. How good it felt to watch it sail into his glove! How good the cheering felt!

> Once again, Donovan is thinking about something else.

"Ice cream?" his mom asked again.

"Sure!" said Donovan with a grin.

DISCUSS What can you tell about Donovan by his speech and actions?

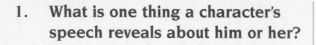

Try These

1. **What is one thing a character's speech reveals about him or her?**

   Ⓐ What the author's personality is like

   Ⓑ What the character's personality is like

   Ⓒ What the character's actions will be

   Ⓓ What the character will do next

   Think about what you learn about people from talking to them.

2. **What would you have to do if you were going to play the role of Donovan in this story?**

   Ⓐ Learn all about what dinosaurs eat.

   Ⓑ Run after you hit the ball.

   Ⓒ Show your attention wandering

   Ⓓ Never listen to what others say.

   Think about what Donovan's actions in the story.

3. **Other than speech, what is the main way an author shows what a character's personality is like?**

   Ⓐ The author tells you about his or her clothing

   Ⓑ The author tells you about his or her actions

   Ⓒ The author tells you what age he or she is

   Ⓓ The author tells you what he or she looks like

4. **What action shows that Donovan finally pays attention and stops daydreaming?**

   Ⓐ He catches the ball and wins the game.

   Ⓑ He decides what flavor ice cream he will have.

   Ⓒ He watches the ball plop on the ground by his feet.

   Ⓓ He forgets to run after he hits the ball.

Lesson 36 — Characters' Motivations

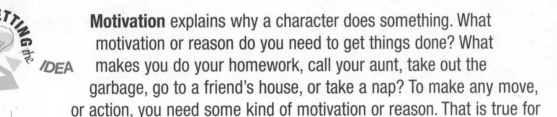

Motivation explains why a character does something. What motivation or reason do you need to get things done? What makes you do your homework, call your aunt, take out the garbage, go to a friend's house, or take a nap? To make any move, or action, you need some kind of motivation or reason. That is true for the characters in books as well.

When you read a story, look and see what motivates the characters to do something. For example, what is this student's motivation?

Jeremy had to do well on this test if he wanted to stay on the team. He went back to studying.

In this case, Jeremy is studying hard so that he can stay on the team. Most likely, he needs to get better grades than he did in the past.

Here is another example:

The wind was increasing and the sky kept getting darker. Linda went outside and started bringing in the clean laundry off the line.

In this example, Linda's motivation for getting the clean laundry off the line is the threat of a storm. She doesn't want the clean clothes to get rained on.

Sometimes motivation can be more complicated. A character could enter a poetry contest because she wants to win the first prize. She also wants others to know that she can write good poetry. In addition, she might want to prove to her friend that writing can be fun and important. Sometimes a character can have more than one reason, or motivation for performing a certain action.

By figuring out why a character is doing something, you will better understand that character's actions.

Example 1

What do you think motivates the character in this next sentence?

The waitress rushed over to the table and served the food quickly.

There is not much information here, but you can make a good guess as to why the waitress is rushing. What could be some possible motivations for this character? Here are a few to get you started:

- She doesn't want the food to get cold.
- It is the end of her shift, and she wants to go home.
- She knows her boss is watching her.
- She knows the customer is impatient.
- She knows the customer is in a rush.

Read the following passage.

The waitress rushed over to the table and served the food quickly. The cook insisted on heating the plates. This time he over did it. The plates were so hot they were burning her hands. As soon as these customers were served, she was going back in the kitchen. Enough was enough. They'd been through this before, but now it was going to stop. "That cook is going to 'cool it' in more ways than one!" she muttered under her breath.

We can also tell that the waitress has a sense of humor. She means "cool it" as "stop it," but she also uses the phrase "cool it" to mean "cool the plates."

This passage explains why the waitress is rushing. She is serving the food quickly because the cook overheated the plates, and this makes her angry. She is going to the kitchen as soon as she serves the food to have a word with the cook.

Example 2

Read this next example. What prediction can you make?

The woman bent over and picked up the two pairs of shoes on the floor.

What could be this woman's motivation for picking up the two pairs of shoes from the floor? Here are a few possibilities:

- She was afraid she would trip over them.
- She wanted to know where they would be in the morning.
- She knew her son would be looking for them tomorrow.
- She wanted to try them on to see if they fit.
- She planned to throw them away because they didn't fit anymore.

Now, let's find out the real reason why the woman was picking up the shoes.

Slowly, the woman bent over and carefully picked up the two pairs of shoes on the floor to put them away. She was tired. It had been a busy day in the shoe department, and she was ready to clean things up and head home. When she got home she would still have to cook dinner for her son. She sighed, thinking of the dirty laundry that needed to be washed and put away. She knew she was lucky to have a job, but that did not make things any easier.

The woman appears to be a saleswoman. She is getting ready go home. Her motivation to pick up the shoes was simple: the sooner she picked them up the shoes and put them away, the sooner she could go home.

We also learn more about this woman's character. She is tired, but when she gets home she will not be able to relax. She has a son who must be fed. She has laundry to be washed. Apparently no one else helps her do these chores. We also learn that she probably has had a hard time. She considers herself lucky to have a job, and this explains why she is so careful when picking up the shoes. She wants to keep her job.

DISCUSS Why does it help to recognize the motivation behind a character's actions in a story?

Try These

1. **What is another word for what motivates a character?**

   (A) Inspiration

   (B) Solution

   (C) Explanation

   (D) Confusion

   If someone is motivated, he or she has a reason to do something.

2. **Why do characters need motivation?**

   (A) It gives them a reason to get things done.

   (B) It is an essential part of the resolution.

   (C) It is the step that comes before setting.

   (D) It provides details about the action.

   All characters have motives for taking certain actions.

3. **What do you need to know before you can understand a character's motivation?**

   (A) Resolution

   (B) Climax

   (C) Details

   (D) The plot

4. **Why does it help you to know what a character's motivation is in a story or passage?**

   (A) It helps you figure out the setting of the story.

   (B) It makes the character's actions easier to understand.

   (C) It gives you clues to how the story will resolve.

   (D) It helps you figure out the story's climax

THE LOST LAKE

by Allen Say

Read Part III of *The Lost Lake*, which describes a father and son's camping trip.

At noontime we stopped by a creek and ate lunch and drank ice-cold water straight from the stream. I threw rocks in the water, and fish, like shadows, darted in the pools.

"Isn't this a good place to camp, Dad?

"I thought we were looking for our lake."

"Yes, right . . . " I mumbled.

The forest went on and on.

"I don't mean to scare you, son," Dad said. "But we're in bear country. We don't want to surprise them, so we have to make a lot of noise. If they hear us, they'll just go away."

What a time to tell me! I started to shout as loudly as I could. Even Dad wouldn't be able to beat off bears. I thought about those people having fun back at the lake. I thought about the creek, too, with all those fish in it. That would have been a fine place to camp. The Lost Lake hadn't been so bad either.

It was dark when we got out of the forest. We built a fire and that made me feel better. Wild animals wouldn't come near a fire. Dad cooked beef stroganoff and it was delicious.

Later it was bedtime. The sleeping bag felt wonderful. Dad and I started to count the shooting stars, then I worried that maybe we weren't going to find our lake.

"What are you thinking about, Luke?" Dad asked.

"I didn't know you could cook like that," I said.

Dad laughed. "That was only freeze-dried stuff. When we get home, I'll cook you something really special."

"You know something, Dad? You seem like a different person up here."

"Better or worse?"

"A lot better."

"How so?"

"You talk more."

"I'll have to talk more often, then."

That made me smile. Then I slept.

Dad shook me awake. The sun was just coming up, turning everything all gold and orange and yellow. And there was the lake, right in front of us.

For a long time we watched the light change on the water, getting brighter and brighter. Dad didn't say a word the whole time. But then, I didn't have anything to say either.

After breakfast we climbed a mountain and saw our lake below us. There wasn't a sign of people anywhere. It really seemed as if Dad and I were all alone in the world.

I liked it just fine.

1. **What event signals the resolution of this story?**

   Ⓐ   They set up camp.

   Ⓑ   They fixed dinner.

   Ⓒ   They went to sleep.

   Ⓓ   They found a lake.

   2.A.1a; 2.A.2b/2.4.01   Plot

2. **What is the theme of this passage?**

   Ⓐ   What supplies you need to go camping

   Ⓑ   How most lakes are too crowded today

   Ⓒ   When it is best to go cross-country

   Ⓓ   A dad and a son reaching their goal

   2.A.1a; 2.A.2b/2.4.01   Theme

3. **What kind of passage is this?**

   Ⓐ   Nonfiction

   Ⓑ   Folktale

   Ⓒ   Fictional story

   Ⓓ   Autobiography

   1.B.1b; 2.A.1b; 2.A.1c/2.4.13   Identifying Genres

4. **What are Luke and his father in this story?**

   Ⓐ   Main characters

   Ⓑ   Supporting characters

   Ⓒ   Themes

   Ⓓ   Plots

   2.A.1a; 2.A.2b/2.4.02 Main and Supporting Characters

5. **Which statement from the passage shows rising action?**

   Ⓐ   "The forest went on and on."

   Ⓑ   "I liked it just fine."

   Ⓒ   "But we're in bear country."

   Ⓓ   "Then I slept."

   2.A.1a; 2.A.2b/2.4.07   Rising Action

6. **What statement from the passage shows the climax?**

Ⓐ "What a time to tell me!"

Ⓑ "It was dark when we got out of the forest."

Ⓒ "That was only freeze-dried stuff."

Ⓓ "And there was the lake, right in front of us."

2.A.1a/ 2.4.07   Climax

7. **Which word best describes how the author portrays the character of Luke at the end of the story?**

Ⓐ Confused

Ⓑ Angry

Ⓒ Satisfied

Ⓓ Tired

2.A.1a; 2.B.1d; 2.A.2a/ 2.4.08   How Characters Are Portrayed

8. **Which trait shows a lot about Luke's dad?**

Ⓐ How he dresses

Ⓑ What he says

Ⓒ Why he camps

Ⓓ Where he works

2.A.1a; 2.A.2a/ 2.4.08   Character's Traits

9. **What is Luke's motivation for going on this trip?**

Ⓐ To spend time with his dad

Ⓑ To find a lost lake

Ⓒ To get some exercise

Ⓓ To try and find a grizzly bear

2.A.1a; 2.B.1c; 2.A.2a/ 2.4.09   Character's Motivation

 Write your answer on a separate sheet of paper. Write your answer in complete sentences. Use the Extended Response Reading Rubric on page 81 to help you write your answer.

10. **Tell which part of the story, "The Lost Lake," is most exciting for you. Then, explain the relationship between the rising action of a story and its climax. Use information from the unit and your own ideas to support your answer.**

2.A.1a; 2.A.2b/ 2.4.01   Rising Action/Climax

Lesson 37 Figurative Language

Some authors use a literary technique called **figurative language** to make their writing richer and more interesting. Figurative language uses words in a special way to be more descriptive. They often make the reader look at common things in unusual ways.

Three techniques, or ways, that many authors use figurative language are: **metaphors**, **similes**, and **idioms**.

Metaphors are comparisons between two things that are not usually alike at all.

The new car was absolute junk.

Similes are comparisons between two unlike things, only they use the words *like* or *as* to show how they are connected.

Her eyes were like sunshine.

Idioms are phrases that normally would not make any sense, yet most people understand exactly what they mean.

It's time to hit the sack.

Coached Reading

Metaphors

A metaphor compares two things that normally would never be linked together.

DIRECTIONS: Read these three metaphors.

My *house* is a black hole.

Normally, a home and a black hole would not be compared. If you read this metaphor in a book, what would you think about this person's house?

Books are tickets to places that don't exist.

This metaphor compares books to tickets. If a character said this in a book, you would know that he or she likes books because they take you to a fictional place.

Flowers are sunshine in a vase.

This metaphor suggests that you can capture sunshine in a vase with flowers.

Writing metaphors is fun! Try writing your own metaphors below.

Homework is _____

Friends are _____.

Libraries are the _____

Love is _____.

Baking cookies is _____

Puppies are _____.

SIMILES

Similes compare two unlike things also. These comparisons use the words *like* or *as*.

DIRECTIONS: Read these five similes.

My brother eats like a bulldozer digging a foundation.

> Of course no one's brother is really a bulldozer. This simile paints a picture in your head of a boy digging away at his food like a giant fork.

Excuses are like belly buttons because everyone has one.

> Are excuses like belly buttons because they look like belly buttons? Why do you think excuses are like belly buttons?

Sunny days in winter are like unexpected treasure.

> Why is this a good comparison? Do you expect to find treasure every day? Think about a typical winter day? Is it dark or sunny?

The days go fast as racecars on a track.

> Why would days be like racecars? What adjective comes to your mind when you picture a racecar?

Maps are like instructions in a foreign language.

> Some people have trouble figuring out how to read a map. Many people have trouble understanding other languages. Can you see how comparing these two problems makes them similar in a certain way?

Writing similes is also fun! Try writing your own similes below.

Trains are like _____.

Vacation is as wonderful as _____.

Saturdays are as fun as _____.

Time passes like _____.

Idioms

Idioms are another kind of figurative language. They mean something quite different from what the actual words themselves mean. Writers will sometimes include them in their writing in order to make conversations sound more real.

DIRECTIONS: Read these six examples. Can you guess the meaning of each idiom?

He has lost his marbles.

> This idiom doesn't literally mean the man lost some small glass balls, it means he went insane.

She will get wind of it.

> This idiom means she will find out something has happened. She will hear about it.

I am tickled pink to see Jose today.

> Do you think the narrator has actually turned pink after seeing Jose? What else could this statement mean?

Don't make a mountain out of a molehill.

> To understand this idiom make the comparison between a mountain and a molehill in your mind. What would someone be doing to a molehill to make it into a mountain?

That name rings a bell.

> You've probably heard this common idiom before. When a bell rings, it is a sign of something being correct, or in this case, someone is recognized or remembered.

I am going home to catch forty winks.

> Can you actually reach your hand out and catch a wink? Imagine a person winking forty times in a row. The narrator is going to take a nap.

Were you familiar with these sayings?
Have you ever read them in a book or magazine article?

Why do authors use figurative language? What purpose does it have?

Try These

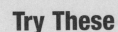

1. Why are idioms hard to learn?

Ⓐ They are long and complicated.

Ⓑ They don't mean what the words actually say.

Ⓒ They compare two unlike things.

Ⓓ They are written in a foreign language.

You have to think hard about the true meaning.

2. Why do writers use figurative language?

Ⓐ To make reading more difficult

Ⓑ To make their writing more interesting

Ⓒ To make readers have to use a dictionary

Ⓓ To frustrate readers

Writing would be boring without similes, metaphors, and idioms.

3. What is the definition of a simile?

Ⓐ A comparison between two unlike things using the words <u>like</u> or <u>as</u>

Ⓑ A comparison between two common things using the words <u>like</u> or <u>as</u>

Ⓒ A technique that helps to establish a story's setting and characters

Ⓓ A technique that demonstrates character's motives and behavior

4. Which of the following is an example of a metaphor?

Ⓐ Her lips were red, ripe cherries.

Ⓑ His hair was like a porcupine.

Ⓒ She was as hungry as a horse.

Ⓓ He was loud as a jackhammer.

Lesson

38 Poetic Devices

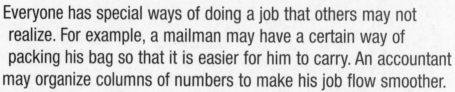

GETTING the IDEA

Everyone has special ways of doing a job that others may not realize. For example, a mailman may have a certain way of packing his bag so that it is easier for him to carry. An accountant may organize columns of numbers to make his job flow smoother. A nurse has a set pattern of tasks that she follows to make sure everything gets done for her patients. Just like other professionals, poets also have specific tricks or devices they use when they are writing their poems. These tricks are called **poetic devices**. The most commonly used devices in poetry are **alliteration**, **onomatopoeia**, **rhyme scheme**, and **consonance**.

Poems usually have far fewer words than a story or article. This means that the poet has to choose each word very carefully and use it well.

For example, if a magazine article about Oregon said:

"Although Oregon gets little snow during the winters, it does get a great deal of rain. Cloud cover is often quite thick, and there are entire weeks without sunshine,"

a poet may write it as:

Sheets of clouds
Wrap around the sun.
Rain is a friend
Who often visits Oregon.

Note that while the subject is the same (Oregon and rain), it is portrayed, or shown, quite differently. The article is stating information to educate, while the poem is giving information to entertain.

Alliteration

If you say *alliteration* a few times, you can feel how it rolls off your tongue. That also partly describes what it is. **Alliteration** is a poetic device where the writer uses words with the same beginning consonant sound in a line or phrase. Think of tongue twisters!

Sally sold sea shells at the sea shore.

Peter Piper picked a peck of pickled peppers.

See how the same sound is repeated in almost every word? Poets use this to get the reader's attention.

Look at the alliteration in this poem.

The Beetles in the garden here
Invite you to the dance, my dear
They plan to celebrate and hop
At the Annual Beetle's Boogie Bop.

> This poem catches your ear with its rhyming words at the end of each line pair. Can you find the alliteration in the last line? There's one that uses "B."

The repetition of the same sound draws attention to the last line. It also makes the poem more fun.

<u>Silly Sam sat</u> in the <u>sand</u>,
<u>While wild Willy waved</u> farewell.
If only Sam met Willy sooner,
<u>Fantastic friends</u> they would be <u>forever</u>.

> This short poem is full of alliteration. Look at the underlined words in each line. They all share the same first consonant with other words in the line.

Onomatopoeia

Here is another word that is very fun to say. It tumbles out of your mouth. Try it!

Onomatopoeia (ah-nah-mah-tah-pee-ah)

It is a fun technique to use as well. The term **onomatopoeia** refers to using words that mean what they sound like. These words excite your ears, and inspire your creativity. Here are some examples:

The clang, crash, and boom of the kitchen pots made her head hurt.

Could you hear the sounds as you read the sentence? The words *clang*, *crash*, and *boom* are all examples of onomatopoeia.

The cat purred as I pet him, but hissed when the mouse in the corner squeaked.

There are three distinct sounds in this sentence: *purred*, *hissed*, and *squeaked*.

Here are a few more examples of words that create sounds when you read.

- Whirr
- Mumble
- Hush

- Boom
- Sputter
- Crackle

- Splash
- Chime
- Kerplunk

Try saying each of these words out loud. Exaggerate them as you say them. GUSHH! BOOOM! …husshhhh… If you listen carefully, you'll hear that the word sounds a lot like the sound it stands for.

Consonance

Both of these poetic devices make a poem come alive and get noticed. First, there is **consonance**. It is alliteration's cousin. Instead of just having the same beginning consonant sound (*Bees bumble in the back*), consonants have the same sounds in any part of the word. For example,

Fred fought fiercely for waffles and coffee.

Notice how the "F" is repeated throughout the line in different places in each: **Fred**, **fought**, **fiercely**, **waffles**, and **coffee**.

Look at these examples:

The singing session was a confession he suggested.

Rhyme Scheme

Rhyme scheme is the term used for poems with words that rhyme (not all of them do!).

Roses are red
Violets are blue
Sugar is sweet
And so are you.

> The "S" sound is at the beginning and middle of many words.

The second and fourth lines rhyme with the words, *blue* and *you*. Other patterns are possible. For example:

I love glue
I truly do
I use it lots
In lines and dots.

> The first and second lines rhyme with the words, *glue* and *do*. What words rhyme in the third and fourth lines?

Here is another example.

Apples crunch,
They taste like fall.
I like to munch,
I eat them all.

> How is this poem different from the last poem you read? In what lines do the rhyming words fall?

Why does it help to know what poetic devices are and how poets use them in their writing?

Try These

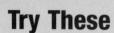

1. **What poetic device uses words like <u>whiz</u> or <u>flash</u>?**

    Ⓐ Onomatopoeia

    Ⓑ Alliteration

    Ⓒ Consonance

    Ⓓ Rhyme scheme

    These are words that create sounds when you read them.

2. **Read this poem. What poetic device does it use?**

    The cars growl

    As they rush by

    The engines roar

    Like caged animals.

    Ⓐ Alliteration

    Ⓑ Onomatopoeia

    Ⓒ Consonance

    Ⓓ Rhyme scheme

    There are no rhymes in this poem, but there are sounds.

3. **Which poetic device is most like alliteration?**

    Ⓐ Onomatopoeia

    Ⓑ Rhyme scheme

    Ⓒ Consonance

    Ⓓ Pattern

4. **How do poetic devices help a poem?**

    Ⓐ They turn it into a tongue twister.

    Ⓑ They make it more exciting and unusual.

    Ⓒ They create longer poems.

    Ⓓ They make each line of the poem rhyme.

PEANUT'S RESCUE

> Read this fictional mystery about a man who loses his best friend and comes to his rescue from a sticky situation.

It hadn't snowed for a few days, but the ground was still blanketed in white from the last big storm. John was taking yet another snowshoe trek through the forest to look for his dog, Peanut. Peanut was a champion show basset hound, but that's not why John missed him. Peanut was a great dog, loyal and loving, and he was the only thing that could make John laugh when he was feeling sad. He'd been feeling very sad ever since Peanut disappeared from his yard the day before yesterday.

Today John took a path he hadn't seen before, calling, "Peanut," the whole way. All of a sudden, he heard barking. Could that be his dog? "Peanut!" he cried, and Peanut barked. He came through a clearing and found Peanut locked in a cage in the front yard of a small house.

"Hey," said John, as he knocked on the door. A small man came out, unsmiling.

"Yeah?" he said.

"That's my dog," said John.

"I don't see any tags on him," said the man. "He's just a stray who wandered to my house the other day. Finders keepers, you know?"

"But he's my dog. Aren't you, Peanut?" Peanut whined and pushed against the side of the cage.

"I guess it's just your word against mine, then," said the man, smiling at last.

John couldn't believe this man could just steal his dog. He couldn't even look at that nasty grin. He hung his head and turned to go, following his snowshoe tracks back to Peanut.

"Tracks," he thought, and started to look around the yard a little. On the ground he could see his own tracks, and the tracks of boots that probably belonged to the man. He could see tracks made by tiny bird feet and by large deer hooves. But he couldn't find any tracks made by the paws of the basset hound.

"He just wandered in?" he asked the man, who was standing at his door, watching.

"That's right."

"Okay then," said John. "Maybe I was wrong," he said, and then turned to his dog and whispered, "Just wait, Peanut. I'll come back for you."

An hour later, he did—with the police. They found Peanuts' tags in the man's trash, along with the tags of some other local dogs who'd been reported missing. The man went to jail.

John went home with his best friend.

1. **What is the climax in the story "Peanut's Rescue"?**

   Ⓐ John knocking on the man's door

   Ⓑ The man saying that he didn't see any tags on Peanut

   Ⓒ John returning with the police to rescue Peanut

   Ⓓ John noticing the tracks in the man's yard

   2.A.1a/2.4.07   Climax

2. **What is John's motivation to keep making the snowshoe treks through the snow?**

   Ⓐ To search for his missing dog, Peanut

   Ⓑ To overcome his sadness

   Ⓒ To get some good exercise

   Ⓓ To find the man's small house

   2.A.1a; 2.B.1c; 2.A.2a/2.4.09   Character's Motivation

3. **Which event marks the start of the rising action in the story, "Peanut's Rescue"?**

   Ⓐ John feeling sad because his dog is missing

   Ⓑ Peanut whining and pushing against the side of his cage

   Ⓒ John hearing his dog bark for the first time

   Ⓓ The police finding the dog tags in the man's trash can

   2.A.1a; 2.A.2b/2.4.07   Rising Action

4. **What is the main idea of a story called?**

   Ⓐ Climax

   Ⓑ Character

   Ⓒ Setting

   Ⓓ Theme

   2.A.a; 2.A.2b/2.4.01   Main Idea

5. **What determines setting in a story other than place?**

    Ⓐ Characters

    Ⓑ Plot

    Ⓒ Time

    Ⓓ Conflict

2.A.1a; 2.A.2b/2.4.01; 2.4.04   Setting

6. **What is a simile?**

    Ⓐ A technique where authors compare two unlike things, using the words *like* or *as*

    Ⓑ A technique poets use to give a rhythm and flow to their poems

    Ⓒ A technique where authors compare two unlike things, without using the words *like* or *as*.

    Ⓓ A technique poets use where all the beginning sounds of the words in a poem are the same

2.A.2a/2.4.11 Similes

7. **How can you recognize the main characters in a story?**

    Ⓐ They are introduced in the first paragraph.

    Ⓑ The story centers on their actions.

    Ⓒ They are usually adults and not children.

    Ⓓ The story points out who they are.

2.A.1a; 2.A.2b/2.4.02   Main and Supporting Characters

8. "Cathy cooks chowder in her crock pot." What poetic device is used in this sentence?

Ⓐ Onomatopoeia

Ⓑ Alliteration

Ⓒ Consonance

Ⓓ Rhyme scheme

2.A.2a /2.4.12   Poetic Devices

9. What is one thing a character's speech reveals about him or her?

Ⓐ What the author's personality is like

Ⓑ What the character's personality is like

Ⓒ What the character's actions will be

Ⓓ What the character will do next

2.A.1a; 2.A.2a/2.4.08; 2.4.10   Character's Speech

 Write your answer on a separate sheet of paper. Write your answer in complete sentences. Use the Extended Response Reading Rubric on page 81 to help you write your answer.

10. You have read many stories in which authors have portrayed characters in many different ways. If an author were going to write a story about your life, how might he or she portray you as a character? Use information from the lesson and your own knowledge to support your answer.

2.A.1a; 2.B.1d; 2.A.2a /2.4.08   How Authors Portray Characters

Now I Can...

Use the skills checklist below to help you complete the "Now I Can . . ." statements.

Now that I understand the different elements of a story, I can connect the details that make up the _____, _____, and _____ to see how it all fits together.

Now I can better understand a story by recognizing how an author portrays his or her characters through their _____ and _____.

Now I can use _____ _____ such as similes and metaphors, to make comparisons in my writing.

...Make the Connection

Place a check in the box before the skill you've mastered.

These are the skills I've learned in this unit:

☐ Plot and subplot

☐ Theme

☐ Character and Setting

☐ Main and Supporting Characters

☐ Rising Action

☐ Climax

☐ How Authors Portray their Characters

☐ Characters' Traits: Speech and Actions

☐ Characters' Motivation

☐ Figurative Language

☐ Poetic Devices

Unit 5 Variety of Literary Works

One of the main reasons that reading is such a wonderful way to spend your time is because there are so many different kinds of literature to choose from. The choices are almost limitless! For instance, you can read about things from the past and then race forward and read about the future. You can also read true stories or tales that are made up. You can learn new skills, improve old ones, and find out about ones you have never heard of before.

In this unit, you will find out what makes a piece of literature a **legend** or **myth**, a true (**nonfiction**) story or pretend (**fiction**) story, and a **folk tale** or a **poem**. Each type of literature is unique and has its own traits. The unit will look at how a poem is put together, how characters make a story come alive, and much more. You will also learn to look at a piece of nonfiction to determine what kind it is and what makes it fit into a particular category.

Try This

Work with a partner. Choose something that each of you has read lately to discuss. It can be a book, story, article, poem, or myth.

- First, summarize the main idea for your partner.
- Then, reverse it so that your partner gives you a summary of what he/she read.
- Discuss how the story would change if the format were different. In other words, if you read a poem, what would it be like as a story? If your partner read a myth, what would it be like as a true story?
- As you discuss each possibility, note what specific traits each type of literature has.

Lesson 39

Myths and Legends

> Can you imagine a time before television, radio, or even books? Even though none of those things existed long ago, the people of that time period still enjoyed a good story. Instead of sitting down to read or watch one, however, they listened to one. Stories were passed down by word of mouth. Good storytellers were honored people. Eager listeners appreciated their skills and could not wait to hear another tale.

Myths

Most of the stories told long ago were either myths or legends. **Myths** are stories that explore the primary beliefs of a culture. They usually center on serious, general themes like love, birth, and death. Most of the time they include powerful superhuman characters. Many myths explore mysterious events like thunder and lightning or the changing of the seasons. Usually myths teach some kind of lesson.

Legends

Legends are similar in that they tie into a culture's history. This time, however, the characters are usually based on actual people such as military leaders and community heroes. Legends can also be based on just plain people like Paul Bunyan.

Myths	Legends
• Superhuman characters	• Mostly human characters
• Symbolic	• Historical
• Extraordinary events	• Often are exaggerated stories
• Cultural	• Cultural

Coached Reading

DIRECTIONS: Read this myth. Look for features of myths or legends.

ORION

This is how Orion was born. One day, Zeus, Hermes, and Poseidon, feeling bored, decided to leave Olympus for a day and go for a walk on earth. Disguised as mortal travelers, they walked all day in the woods and fields until they were footsore and hungry. They called at the house of a poor farmer, Hyrieus, and asked him to give them something to eat. Hyrieus was a kind and generous man. He made the travelers welcome. Since he had no other food in the house, he decided to serve his only ox to make their evening meal.

> After reading this paragraph, we know that this story is a myth because the characters are superhuman.

After they had eaten, the travelers revealed themselves as gods. "As a reward for your kindness," Zeus said to Hyrieus, "ask for any gift you like, and it will be yours."

"My lord," said Hyrieus, "the only gift I want in all the world is a son of my own. But, I'm afraid that it cannot be. My wife has been dead and buried for many years."

"This is what you must do," said Zeus. "Take that ox-skin and bury it in your garden. After nine months, it will turn into a handsome son." Then he touched the skin with his royal staff, and the three gods disappeared into the evening sky.

Hyrieus buried the ox-skin as he had been told. For nine long months, he waited impatiently. Finally, one day, while he was standing on the spot where the skin had been, he found a newborn baby. Hyrieus named him Orion.

> This is a very extraordinary event. This is another clue that the passage is a myth.

Orion grew up strong and proud. He was a skillful hunter, and often used to go out into the countryside to look for game. When he was grown up he left his father Hyrieus and set out to see the world. Wherever he went he was sure to go hunting in the local forests and mountainsides. Soon, his fame spread all around the world.

One day, while he was hunting on the island of Crete, he met Artemis, the hunting goddess. For days they hunted together, tracking the wild beasts of the hills and woods. Orion was very delighted with Artemis and very proud of his own hunting skills. One day, he decided to do something really unusual to surprise her. He went hunting by himself all day, and when Artemis came to find him in the evening, he proudly showed her a huge heap of dead animals and birds. "There Artemis!" he said. "In your honor, I've killed every living thing on Crete."

Unfortunately, Orion didn't know that Artemis, as well as being the goddess of hunting, was also the protector of all wild animals and birds. She looked at the pile of wasted bodies and stamped her foot angrily on the ground. At once an enormous scorpion sprang up out of the earth. "Hunt that, Orion!" she said.

Orion lifted his bow. But he was too slow. The scorpion arched its venomous sting and killed him. Artemis looked down at his body. "To hunt a few animals for sport is allowed," she said. "But to kill everything in sight is proud and foolish." And she set the scorpion among the stars, to remind men forever about the risks of pride.

DISCUSS What lesson does the Greek myth "Orion" teach? What mysterious thing does it explain?

Try These

1. **Where did stories come from before books existed?**

   Ⓐ Television

   Ⓑ Radio

   Ⓒ Magazines

   Ⓓ Storytellers

   Think about history and time order. What would have come before books?

2. **What is the main point of most myths and legends?**

   Ⓐ To explain something about a culture's history

   Ⓑ To show how gods and goddesses behave

   Ⓒ To honor past military leaders and heroes

   Ⓓ To explain how constellations are created

   Remember that the question is about both myths and legends.

3. **Who are the main characters in a myth?**

   Ⓐ Military leaders

   Ⓑ Humans

   Ⓒ Gods

   Ⓓ Animals

4. **Who are the main characters in a legend?**

   Ⓐ Goddesses

   Ⓑ Animals

   Ⓒ Real people

   Ⓓ Families

Lesson 40 Stories

GETTING the IDEA

Stories are fictional tales. This means that stories are made up by the writer and share the same basic elements. The first one is **character**. Many authors create fascinating characters that seem very real. Characters can include animals, robots, and of course, humans. Can you remember any characters from stories that you have read in the past?

Stories take place at a certain location at a certain time. This is called the **setting**. Remembering the details of the setting is important and can help you to better understand the story.

Stories also have a beginning, middle, and end. This is called **story structure**. In addition, a **plot** connects all of the characters and events in a story together. The plot is the sequence of events in a story.

Look at the left diagram below. If your life were a story, what would go in the setting, characters, structure, and plot boxes?

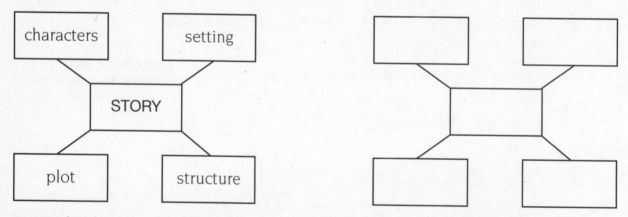

Using the diagram on the right, write specific details of your life in the setting, plot, and story structure boxes.

Coached Reading

DIRECTIONS: Read the story. As you do, identify the setting, plot, characters, and story structure.

THE COLT

by Gertrude Sellon

There was once a young colt who lived on the moor with the other horses. One day, he decided that he was going to go for a run down the road.

"Stay here on the moor," an old horse told him.

"Why?" the colt asked.

"I do not know. I have always been told to stay by the old horses, so you should do the same. Do not leave the moor," he responded.

The colt snorted at him and went running down the road. Soon he met an old mare standing near an inn. "What are you doing out here?" she asked. "You should go back to the moor!"

"No!" replied the colt. "You and the old horse just don't want me to have any fun, that's all!" With that, he left and galloped farther down the road. Soon he met a mule, who also told him to go back to the moor. Again, the colt said no. He ran and ran until he reached town.

When he got there, he was very surprised and bewildered. Who were all of these people? Why was there so much noise? What were all of these carts doing here? He began to feel quite crazy!

> This paragraph introduces the characters—a young colt and some older horses—and identifies the setting, a moor. A moor is an open field.

> Look for sentences that begin and end with quotation marks. Quotation marks show that someone is talking. Fiction often includes conversation between characters.

> Each of these paragraphs creates the tension of the story. For some reason all the horses must stay on the moor, but this young colt disobeys. What do you think will happen to him?

Then some men and boys began chasing him. Everyone shouted at him. Finally, he saw another horse, and he ran up to it, asking what was going on. The other horse did not answer, so the colt tried to hit him with his head. Unfortunately, the colt was talking to his own reflection in a store window!

The colt's head was cut open, and he was scared. Suddenly, his owner appeared. "What is my colt doing here so far away from the moor?" he asked. "He's not to be trusted, I guess."

Here we learn about what lies beyond the moor, and the possible dangers there. Is there danger? Does the colt meet harm in any way?

That night, the colt returned to the moor, with his head bandaged and a thick log chained to his leg to keep him from running away again. Never again did he run away, and when he grew into an old horse, he always told the young colts, "Never, never, never leave the moor!"

Pay attention to how stories end. The ending will usually show how characters changed. Did the colt learn anything from his adventures?

DISCUSS What are the two settings of this story? Which setting do the horses prefer?

Try These

1. **What was the setting at the beginning of the story?**

   Ⓐ A town

   Ⓑ A house

   Ⓒ A city

   Ⓓ A moor

   Think about which place the colt is told not to leave.

2. **Who is not a character in the story?**

   Ⓐ The colt

   Ⓑ A mule

   Ⓒ The colt's owner

   Ⓓ The moor

   Think about which of these choices is not a living creature.

3. **After which event does the owner find the colt?**

   Ⓐ After the colt's leg is chained to a log

   Ⓑ After the men and boys chased the colt

   Ⓒ After the colt cut his head on the store window

   Ⓓ After the colt talks to the old horse

4. **What is the word that describes a story's sequence of events?**

   Ⓐ Setting

   Ⓑ Character

   Ⓒ Plot

   Ⓓ Structure

Lesson 41

Folk Tales

GETTING the IDEA

You may have heard of "Little Red Riding Hood," "The Three Little Pigs," or "Rapunzel." These are all examples of folk tales (sometimes called fairy tales). Folk tales are similar to myths and legends. They have been around for a very long time and were once shared by word of mouth. Often they begin with the familiar phrases such as:

"Once upon a time"   "A long time ago"
"There once was"   "Many years ago"

Folk tales come from countries all over the world. Many countries have very similar folk tales that share similar themes. For example, the story of a little girl who is tricked by a wolf is known as "Lon Po Po" in China, "Little Red Cap" in Germany, and "Little Red Riding Hood" in France.

Other familiar titles you might recognize are "Beauty and the Beast," "Sleeping Beauty," "Hansel and Gretel," and "Snow White and the Seven Dwarves"

In folk tales, there are always good characters and evil characters. In these tales, good characters almost always win against evil, and there is usually a happy ending. The table below shows some common elements of folktales.

Folk tales				
Begins with: "Once upon a time," or "A long time ago"	Passed down through storytellers	Also called fairy tales	Good wins against evil or a lesson is taught	Usually end happily

Coached Reading

DIRECTIONS: Read the following folk tale. Think about the elements of folk tales.

THE STRAW, THE COAL, AND THE BEAN

by the Brothers Grimm

A long time ago, there lived a poor old woman who had very little. She gathered some beans for dinner, and then made a fire to cook them. She put a handful of straw onto the fire to make it burn quicker, and then put the pot of beans over it.

> Notice how the tale begins. The story is set a long time ago.

Soon after, a piece of straw fell out of the inglenook (a corner by a fireplace). A moment later, a small coal shot out and landed beside the piece of straw. Next to them was a bean that dropped out of the pot.

The three talked for a moment and then realized that each had just escaped death. "If we do not leave here, the old woman will toss us back on the fire to burn!" cried the straw. The three decided to be friends, and they left the house. They walked for a while until they came to a small stream.

> Another common feature of folktales is having characters that are not human but take on human characteristics, such as walking and talking.

"How will we get across?" asked the bean.

"I know!" said the straw. "I will lie down and act as a bridge so that you two can cross over. Then you can pull me up from the other side." So the straw got down and spread across the water. The coal started out across the straw, but when he reached the middle of the stream, he got frightened. In fact, he was so scared that he couldn't move!

While the coal stood there, motionless, the straw began to feel hot. Then he realized he was burning! The coal burned him straight through the center, and both he and the coal fell into the cold water and disappeared.

The bean thought that this was very funny. He laughed so hard that he actually burst in two!

A passing tailor saw the bean and felt sorry for him. He pulled out his black thread and sewed the bean back up. The bean went on to live a long life, but it never got rid of its scar. To this day, all beans still have a black seam.

> The story ends happily for the bean.

DISCUSS In the folk tale on page 237, what mystery is solved about beans? Do you think this tale is true? Why or why not.

Try These

1. **What do folk tales told around the world have in common?**

Ⓐ They have the same theme.

Ⓑ They have the same character names.

Ⓒ They have the same titles.

Ⓓ They have the same authors.

Think about the lesson in "Little Red Riding Hood."

2. **Which character helps the bean at the end of this tale?**

Ⓐ The old woman

Ⓑ The coal

Ⓒ The straw

Ⓓ The tailor

Go back and read the end of the tale. Think about which character feels sorry for the bean.

3. **What phrase would you use to introduce a folk tale?**

Ⓐ "In the year 1812"

Ⓑ "On Tuesday"

Ⓒ "Once upon a time"

Ⓓ "One year ago"

Write your answer on a separate sheet of paper. Write your answer in complete sentences. Use the Extended Response Reading Rubric on page 81 to help you write your answer.

4. **What lesson does "The Straw, the Coal, and the Bean" teach the reader? Why do you think this tale was told? Use information from the passage and your own ideas to support your answer.**

Lesson 42 Nonfiction

GETTING the IDEA

Folk tales, stories, legends, and myths are fictional stories, which means that they are made up. **Nonfiction**, on the other hand, is just the opposite. Nonfiction pieces are true writings about real people and real events.

Nonfiction writing can be in many different forms. Here are a few examples:

Expository nonfiction pieces share information with the reader. They are a little like news reports. They give you real information and facts. For example, an expository piece might tell you about a moment in history or about a recent study on polar bears.

Persuasive nonfiction pieces try to convince a reader to make a certain decision or take a certain action. They are similar to television commercials. A television commercial tries to get you to buy something. Likewise, a persuasive piece of nonfiction tries to get you to agree with what it says.

Lastly, **functional (instructional) nonfiction** pieces tell you how to do or make something. For example, television stations that show you how to fix up an old house or make a couch pillow, are functional. Functional nonfiction can also give you information, such as when the bus gets to your corner or what time you must get to ball practice.

For example, let's say the topic is getting a library card. An **expository** piece would detail what a library card membership might cost, what rights it gives you, and what types of books are available for checkout. A **functional** piece would explain a step-by-step process on how to apply for a library card, while a **persuasive** piece would list all of the great reasons why every person should have his or her own library card.

Coached Reading

DIRECTIONS: Read the following three nonfiction passages. Notice how each approaches the topic from a different angle.

Expository Nonfiction

According to several studies, more than 90 million people are interested in taking care of birds on their property. Some of them have birdfeeders hanging from their trees, while others have birdhouses. A number of them also have bird baths for when birds need a little freshening up. Bird watching is quickly becoming one of the nation's most popular hobbies, and many watchers like to see birds stopping by in their own back yards.

> This passage gives information and facts about people's interest in birds. This is an expository piece because it gives you details about birds, birdfeeders, birdhouses, and bird watchers.

Functional (or Instructional) Nonfiction

Tools: Hammer, nails, wood, saw, paint, sandpaper, pencil, and tape measurer.

1. Mount the birdhouse six to ten feet high in a tree.
2. If you build more than one birdhouse on your property, try to space them 20 to 50 feet apart.
3. After you have plotted out where to locate the birdhouses, you can assemble the tools listed below into one place.
4. Place the pattern for the project on a flat surface and you will be ready to begin.

> This passage instructs the reader on where to place birdhouses on his or her property. It will also explain how to build a birdhouse. This is a functional (or instructional) piece because it takes you through a step-by-step process on how to do something.

Persuasive Nonfiction

If you care about the well-being of our fine, feathered friends, you must build a birdhouse in your backyard. This gives all kinds of bird species a place to use for shelter when the weather or the seasons change. Installing birdfeeders throughout your property is just as important. A birdbath can also be a wonderful addition to your yard. It gives birds a chance to clean their feathers and take a welcome break. Birdhouses, feeders, and baths are all thoughtful things to put in your yard, and they help the world to be a better place.

> This is a persuasive piece because it is trying to persuade the reader to do something--place birdhouses, birdfeeders, and birdbaths in his or her yard. It states that placing these items in a yard will help the bird live a happier, healthier life.

DISCUSS Which kind of nonfiction would be best for finding information on life in South America? Explain why.

Try These

1. **Which kind of nonfiction would instruct you on how to make a new kind of food?**

   Ⓐ Narrative

   Ⓑ Functional

   Ⓒ Persuasive

   Ⓓ Expository

   Think about the passage's purpose. Will it give you information? Will it tell you how to do something? Will it try to convince you of something?

2. **Which kind of nonfiction would try to convince you that soccer is better than other sports?**

   Ⓐ Narrative

   Ⓑ Functional

   Ⓒ Persuasive

   Ⓓ Expository

   Think about what the passage tried to do. Did it give you information? Did it tell you how to do something? Did it try to convince you of something?

3. **Which passage tells you that 90 million people are interested in taking care of birds?**

   Ⓐ Narrative

   Ⓑ Functional

   Ⓒ Persuasive

   Ⓓ Expository

    Write your answer on a separate sheet of paper. Write your answer in complete sentences. Use the Extended Response Reading Rubric on page 81 to help you write your answer.

4. **Your teacher tells you that you have to write a book report in order to convince people to read a book. Write three sentences to convince people to read a book. Use information from this lesson and your own ideas to support your answer.**

Lesson

43 Poetry

Poetry comes in different types and lengths. Some poems are very short, while others, called **epic poems**, are quite long and tell an entire story. It is important to remember that poems can have various themes. A **theme** is the subject or message of a text.

Read this excerpt from a poem that rhymes and has a very simple theme.

All day long I heard that song,
Trying to tell me what was right and wrong.
All night long, I had only one fine dream,
Making me hungry for ice cream.

Common Elements of Poetry

Element	Description
Length	Although a poem can be of different lengths, its individual lines are usually shorter than normal sentences.
Rhyme	Some poems rhyme, while others do not. Those that do, usually have ending words that rhyme in a variety of patterns. Those that do not rhyme still have a rhythm, which can be heard when read aloud.
Stanzas	When reading other kinds of writing, ideas are gathered together in paragraphs. In poetry, ideas are put together in groups called stanzas.
Specific Words	Since poetry uses shorter lines and has a particular rhythm, each word is chosen very carefully. Many are chosen for the sounds they make or the number of syllables they have. 1. **Onomatopoeia** is used for words that sound like what they mean. For example, words like *buzz*, *hiss*, *pop*, and *clang*, are all examples of onomatopoeia. 2. **Alliteration** is used when a consonant sound is repeated in a line. For example, the sentence, "The spirited song saved the sailors," is an example of alliteration.

Coached Reading

DIRECTIONS: Read the following poems. Each one illustrates different elements of poetry.

SONG OF THE FISHES

Come all you bold fishermen, listen to me
I'll sing you a song of the fish of the sea.
So blow, ye winds westerly, westerly blow,
We're bound to the southward, so stead we go.

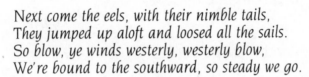

First comes the blue-fish a-wagging his tail,
He comes up on deck and yells: "All hands make sail."
So blow, ye winds westerly, westerly blow,
We're bound to the southward, so stead we go.

Every two lines has a different rhyme.

Next come the eels, with their nimble tails,
They jumped up aloft and loosed all the sails.
So blow, ye winds westerly, westerly blow,
We're bound to the southward, so steady we go.

THUMBPRINT

by Eve Merriam

In the heel of my thumb
are whorls, whirls, wheels
in a unique design;
mine alone.
What a treasure to own!
My own flesh, my own feelings.
No other, however, grand or base,
can ever contain the same.
My signature,
thumbing the pages of my time.
My universe key,
my singularity.
Impress, implant,
I am myself,
of all my atom parts I am the sum.
And out of my blood and my brain
I make my own interior weather,
my own sun and rain.
Imprint my mark upon the world,
whatever I shall become.

Here is an example of alliteration.

DISCUSS How does a message change when it is put in the form of a poem instead of in the form of a story or essay?

Try These

1. Which of the following sentences contains an example of alliteration?

Ⓐ We went walking with the winners.

Ⓑ The cars whiz by with a blast of air.

Ⓒ I like carrots and I like parrots.

Ⓓ Star-light, star-bright

Remember that alliteration is a series of words beginning with the same sound.

2. What is the theme of "Song of the Fishes?"

Ⓐ Blue fish in the sea

Ⓑ Eels in the sea

Ⓒ Sailing on the sea

Ⓓ Winds over the sea

The theme is not stated in words. The theme is implied. Think about what the fishes are singing about.

3. What are long poems that tell a story called?

Ⓐ Stanzas

Ⓑ Epics

Ⓒ Poetry

Ⓓ Rhyme

4. "There was a huge <u>boom</u> and suddenly the <u>whisper</u> of the wind became a moaning <u>clatter</u>." What are the underlined words examples of?

Ⓐ Alliteration

Ⓑ Onomatopoeia

Ⓒ Rhyme

Ⓓ Epic

A CHANCE TO SEE

This passage explains the steps of an eye exam.

People of all ages need help in being able to see clearly. Some of them wear glasses, while others wear contact lenses. Before they can get either one, they have to have an eye examination.

A thorough eye examination involves many different steps. It often takes about an hour to complete and requires a specially trained doctor called an opthalmologist. The patient has to look through a large variety of lenses to see which helps him or her to see better and which ones do not. He may also have to look at some charts and answer a lot of questions about what he can and cannot see.

Once the examination is complete, the doctor will discuss what kind of help is needed. He will usually tell you about the advantages and disadvantages of glasses and contacts. They each have their own benefits, and usually, the decision comes down to appearance and convenience. He may also recommend bifocals or trifocals for certain patients. After the choice has been made, the prescription is ordered. Once the glasses or contacts are in, the patient returns to the doctor's office to try them on and make sure they are comfortable.

Being able to see well is vital for people of all ages. A thorough examination with a skillful doctor can lead everyone to seeing the world clearly!

TESTING TIME

This is a poem about an eye examination.

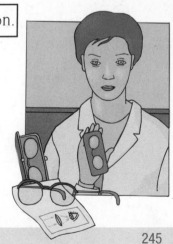

Squint and blink, water and wink
Is it time to rest from this test?
He steps in and with a grin,
Says look again, and tell me when
You can see most clearly.
I whisper yes, that's my best guess,
And he says good, it's understood,
So let's proceed to the glasses you need.

1. **What kind of story is "A Chance to See"?**

   Ⓐ Persuasive nonfiction

   Ⓑ Expository nonfiction

   Ⓒ Functional nonfiction

   Ⓓ Folk tale

   1.B.1b; 2.A.1b/2.4.13; 2.4.14   Identifying Genre

2. **How many stanzas are there in the poem "Testing Time"?**

   Ⓐ 1

   Ⓑ 2

   Ⓒ 3

   Ⓓ 8

   1.B.1b; 2.A.1b; 2.A.1c/2.4.13   Poetry

3. **What kind of story often has characters based on real people?**

   Ⓐ Myth

   Ⓑ Fable

   Ⓒ Folk tale

   Ⓓ Legend

   1.B.1b; 2.A.1b; 2.A.1c/2.4.13   Identifying Genres

4. **What is the beginning, middle and end of a story called?**

   Ⓐ The plot

   Ⓑ The setting

   Ⓒ The structure

   Ⓓ The characters

   1.B.1b; 2.A.1b; 2.A.1c/2.4.13   Stories

5. **What kind of story often has main characters that are superhuman?**

   Ⓐ Poetry

   Ⓑ Nonfiction

   Ⓒ Myth

   Ⓓ Legends

   1.B.1b; 2.A.1b; 2.A.1c/2.4.13   Identifying Genres

 Write your answer on a separate sheet of paper. Write your answer in complete sentences. Use the Extended Response Reading Rubric on page 81 to help you write your answer.

6. **Explain what a folk tale is by listing three things that make up a folk tale. Give two examples of a folk tale. Use information from the unit and your own ideas to support your answer.**

   1.B.1b; 2.A.1b; 2.A.1c/2.4.13   Folk tales

Now I Can...

Use the skills checklist below to help you complete the "Now I Can . . ." statements.

Now that I know that a good _____ has a setting, characters, and a plot, I can use what I know to write my own narratives.

Now that I can tell the difference between _____ nonfiction (writing used to persuade) and _____ nonfiction (writing used to explain things) I can figure out a writer's purpose for writing nonfiction.

Now that I know how to use onomatopoeia and alliteration, I can create _____ with its own unique rhythm.

...Make the Connection

Place a check in the box before the skill you've mastered.

These are the skills I've learned in this unit:

☐ Myths and Legends

☐ Stories

☐ Folk Tales

☐ Nonfiction

☐ Poetry

☐ Expository nonfiction

☐ Persuasive nonfiction

☐ Functional (instructional) nonfiction

Posttest

Session 1

A NIGHT AT HOYT CASTLE

Read this fictional story about a traveler who finds himself staying in spooky quarters one cold, stormy night in February.

The howling wind outside forced the fire in the fireplace to grow and shrink. This made the shadows on the wall expand and recede. I pulled the blankets up over my head, willing myself to sleep.

Sleep was impossible, however. My mind raced. Why had I agreed to stop here, of all places? Why, in fact, had I agreed to travel on these back roads in February? Another few inches of snow would close the pass for good. The thought of being stuck here for weeks made me shudder.

I rose and looked out the window. Sleet slammed against the stones of the castle. The wind made the sleet move horizontally, and it looked as though the sky were streaked with light. The stone floor was freezing cold, and the fire barely reached my four-poster bed in the corner of the dark, damp room. A shutter slammed against the window, and I leaped for the safety of the bed.

1   Which of the following words from the passage contains a prefix?

Ⓐ   Howling

Ⓑ   Impossible

Ⓒ   Travel

Ⓓ   Window

2. Which of the following words from the passage is a compound word?

Ⓐ   Expand

Ⓑ   Inches

Ⓒ   Fireplace

Ⓓ   Castle

3. Which phrase from the passage contains a context clue for an unfamiliar word?

Ⓐ   I pulled the blankets up over my head…

Ⓑ   The stone floor was freezing cold…

Ⓒ   The wind made the sleet move horizontally…

Ⓓ   The thought of being stuck here for weeks made me shudder…

4. To which of these words from the passage could you add the suffix -<u>ful</u> to make a new word?

Ⓐ   Sleep

Ⓑ   Thought

Ⓒ   Shudder

Ⓓ   Safety

5. What is the word root in <u>unreachable</u>?

Ⓐ   Un

Ⓑ   Re

Ⓒ   Reach

Ⓓ   Able

GO ON TO THE NEXT PAGE

A SMOOTH WALKER

by Tamra Orr

> Read this informational passage about robots. Robots may help make our lives much easier someday soon.

Today, most robots are still mostly seen in science fiction movies or read about in books, but not for long. Scientists from countries like the U.S., Japan, and the Netherlands are working hard to build real robots. They hope that one day these robots will be able to do everything from household chores to going into outer space to clean up toxic, or deadly, waste.

Scientists face many different challenges as they work to create robots. One of the biggest problems scientists are working to overcome is in how to make robots walk like people do. It is much harder than most people think. Have you ever stopped to consider how many body systems are involved in your taking just one step? Your brain must send the message to the muscles in your hips, thighs, calves, and feet to get them to move. It takes a lot of different things happening at just the right time for people to stay balanced and walk easily. Scientists try to recreate this sequence of events mechanically. Some of the early robot models walked like penguins. They are getting better.

One robot, built by the Massachusetts Institute of Technology, is just over one foot tall and weighs about six pounds. It has curved feet. It is called "The Toddler" because of the way it walks. It puts all of its weight on one foot before moving the other. So far, it can start, stop, steer itself in different directions and even walk backwards.

6. **What is a synonym of <u>difficult</u>?**

   (A) Serious

   (B) Confusing

   (C) Hard

   (D) Important

7. **What is an antonym of <u>different</u>?**

   (A) Variety

   (B) Same

   (C) Detailed

   (D) Essential

8. **Which word from the passage is a homonym?**

   (A) Seen

   (B) Foot

   (C) Designed

   (D) Long

9. **What does the word <u>toxic</u> mean?**

   (A) Pleasant

   (B) Deadly

   (C) Fresh

   (D) Functional

10. **Which set of words contains homonyms?**

    (A) Heed/Head

    (B) Cool/Warm

    (C) Laugh/Giggle

    (D) Weighs/Ways

GO ON TO THE NEXT PAGE ➡

AMELIA EARHART

This is an expository passage about a brave woman named Amelia Earhart. Amelia made history by being the first woman to fly across the Atlantic Ocean.

In the 1920s and 1930s, women in the United States usually were not as famous as men. This was because most women stayed home and did not work. Women who worked usually had jobs that were traditionally held by women, such as teachers and nurses. Some female pioneers (a pioneer is someone who is the first to accomplish something), refused to act like other women of the time. They wanted to do something important and fun. One of these women was named Amelia Earhart.

As a young woman living during World War I, Amelia worked as a nurse in a military hospital. Then she went to school to study medicine. While visiting her family in California, she went to an air show. She was fascinated by the airplanes. The next day, she went for a short flight in an open-cockpit plane. She was hooked. Amelia decided that she wanted to be a pilot.

She stopped studying medicine and started learning how to fly a plane. Her teacher was a female pilot named Anita Snook. After learning to fly, Amelia traveled for a while, making news in different cities. Most people had never heard of a woman who could fly a plane!

In 1927, Charles Lindbergh was the first person to fly solo (alone) across the Atlantic Ocean. A year later, Amelia was the first woman to fly across the Atlantic, although she did not actually fly the plane—she was only a passenger. Two men named Wilmer Stultz and Slim Gordon piloted the plane. The press did not care. All of the newspapers said Amelia was the first woman to cross the Atlantic. They started calling her "Lady Lindy," after Charles Lindbergh. This upset her, because she didn't really fly the plane. She decided to correct this misunderstanding. A few years later, in 1932, she was the first woman to fly solo across the Atlantic.

Even though she had been very successful as a pilot, Amelia had one dream. She wanted to be the first woman to fly around the world. In 1937, she and a copilot, Frederick Noonan, took off from Oakland, California on the first leg of their trip. From there they flew to Miami, Florida, and then to Puerto Rico. Then they flew down to South America, and across the ocean to Africa and the Red Sea, and then on to Asia. While they were flying from Asia to Australia, their plane disappeared. Nobody knows where they went or what happened to them. Even though we do not know what happened to this amazing woman, she is till widely admired for her many courageous accomplishments.

11. **In 1992, a plane that some people believe was Amelia Earhart's was found on an island in the Pacific Ocean. What most likely happened on her flight?**

    Ⓐ She saw the island and decided to land to do some sight-seeing.

    Ⓑ She had engine trouble and landed on the island to make repairs.

    Ⓒ She was hungry and landed on the island to get food.

    Ⓓ She was lonely and landed on the island to meet people.

12. **Which of the following is an implicit main idea from this passage?**

    Ⓐ Women did not have the same opportunities as men in the 1920s and 1930s.

    Ⓑ Most people who served in World War I eventually became airplane pilots.

    Ⓒ Amelia Earhart was first to fly solo across the Atlantic.

    Ⓓ No one knows what happened to Amelia Earhart and her co-pilot.

13. **Why did Amelia love flying?**

    Ⓐ She was paid a lot of money.

    Ⓑ She thought that flying was fun and exciting.

    Ⓒ She was scared of heights.

    Ⓓ She needed a job.

14. **What would most likely have happened if Amelia Earhart survived a crash before she left Oakland?**

    Ⓐ She would have decided to be a nurse instead.

    Ⓑ She would have boarded another plane and tried again.

    Ⓒ She would have given up.

    Ⓓ She would have decided to become a race car driver.

15. **Which of the following is an explicit main idea from this passage?**

    Ⓐ Amelia Earhart was jealous of Anita Snook's success.

    Ⓑ Amelia Earhart and her co-pilot flew around the world.

    Ⓒ Amelia Earhart was determined to be a pilot.

    Ⓓ Amelia Earhart was a doctor before she was a pilot.

GO ON TO THE NEXT PAGE

GOING TO THE PARK FOR SCHOOL

by Tamra Orr

> Read this informational passage about an outdoor school in Africa. The school's theme is based around nature. Imagine what it would be like to go to school outside everyday!

The children that go to South Africa's Southern Cross School have to make sure they dress for the weather. At this school, classrooms are outside. Lessons are pulled more from the nature around them than from books.

Learning About The Environment

The *motto*, or short saying that states the theme of the school, is "A School for the Planet." It can be found on matching green hats and t-shirts worn by the children. The teachers here still have to follow the same lessons as in other schools throughout Africa. They just depend on nature to give them most of the teaching tools they will need.

Preschoolers learn to count by seeing how many animal tracks they can name near the water *trough* where the animals come to drink. Higher levels of math might be taught by asking the children to figure out how much water is gone. Then they figure out how much will be used in a day, a week or a month.

Class With The Animals

This school is located near a national park. More than 100 children come to school by walking along the Warthog Trot. It is not unusual to share the trail with a giraffe or other African animals like *wildebeests* and *impalas*. The grass is kept short by hungry warthogs. The class pet is a large snake that was hurt. The children in the class are helping it to get better. Then it will be let go. Huts turn into the classrooms on days where the weather is bad or it is time to do some desk work.

Students at the South African Cross School see giraffes like this one everyday—in their own classrooms!

All subjects are taught at this school, but the teachers highlight **environmental issues**. Reading, writing, and speech are often tied into subjects about nature. Children will leave school with a true understanding of how nature works!

16. **What graphic is used in this passage to tell what each section will be about?**

    Ⓐ Captions

    Ⓑ Italics

    Ⓒ Bold print

    Ⓓ Subheadings

17. **What graphic is used in this passage to help you understand unfamiliar vocabulary?**

    Ⓐ Italics

    Ⓑ Bold print

    Ⓒ Subtitles

    Ⓓ Charts

18. **Which of the following graphic organizers would help you compare schools in the U.S.A. and South Africa's Southern Cross?**

    Ⓐ Pie chart

    Ⓑ Venn diagram

    Ⓒ Bar graph

    Ⓓ Photo caption

19. **How do photo captions help you to understand what you are reading?**

    Ⓐ They give you important facts and statistics about the topic.

    Ⓑ They link the passage information to the visual pictures.

    Ⓒ They tell you what the next section is going to be about.

    Ⓓ They provide essential details about the author of the passage.

20. **How is bold print used in this passage?**

    Ⓐ To explain a photograph

    Ⓑ To tell who wrote the article

    Ⓒ To stress an important or new idea

    Ⓓ To draw attention to a graph

GO ON TO THE NEXT PAGE ➡

THE NEW GIRL

This is a story about a shy girl named Angela who overcomes her shyness to make a new friend.

Angela walked quickly through the hall with her head down. She didn't speak to anyone; she almost never spoke in school. If someone greeted her, she would smile and look at the ground; if a teacher called on her in class, she would blush and have trouble answering, even though she almost always got the answer right.

In her classroom, Angela was making her way to her seat when she noticed a new girl with short brown hair and very bright blue eyes sitting in the seat next to hers. The girl smiled at Angela and said, "Hello, I'm Trudy, and I'm new here. What's your name?" She had a British accent.

Angela took a deep breath, thinking that this girl was someone she would really like to know. She wanted very badly to talk to Trudy, and she forced the words out: "I'm Angela."

"That's a pretty name, much better than mine, which is really Gertrude," Trudy said. "We just moved here, to this town — well, really, we just moved to this country! I cannot believe how incredibly hot it is here. I'm not used to that because at home, it rains all the time, and it's very cool. Does it ever rain here?"

Angela smiled. "Sometimes it does, in the spring, and then all the wildflowers come out. Usually it's pretty dry, though; that's why we have the desert, you know."

Trudy made a face and said, "I'll bet you think I'm a real idiot for not knowing that! Maybe you could show me the desert one of these days?"

21. **What information in the passage shows that Angela is smart?**

    (A) She blushes.

    (B) She gets the answers right.

    (C) She doesn't speak.

    (D) She walks quickly.

22. **What is the main idea of the first paragraph?**

    (A) Angela is British.

    (B) Angela lives near a desert.

    (C) Angela is shy.

    (D) Angela has many friends.

23. **What detail supports the inference that Trudy is from England?**

    (A) She has a British accent.

    (B) It rains a lot in her country.

    (C) She says "hello" first.

    (D) She says she is from England.

24. **What is the best definition of an inference?**

    (A) An explicit idea

    (B) A concept the author does not actually state

    (C) A summary of the main idea

    (D) A gathering of the story's supporting details

25. **What is another word for a story's main idea?**

    (A) Subplot

    (B) Theme

    (C) Details

    (D) Setting

GO ON TO THE NEXT PAGE ➡

NOTICE: Photocopying any part of this book is prohibited by law.

259

This is a flyer used to inform students of an upcoming talent show. Flyers are an easy way to distribute information around a community, like your school.

COME TO THE SPRING TALENT SHOW!

You won't want to miss it.
Saturday, May 9 from 7:00 P.M. to 9:30 P.M.

Be surprised at what your friends and teachers can do!
Who can sing? Who can dance? Who can act? Who can juggle?
Is there a superstar hiding inside one of us?

Tickets are only $3 per person. Half of that money
goes to buying new uniforms for the track team.
BRING YOUR WHOLE FAMILY!

Here is the line-up for this Night of Fun:

7:00 P.M. Students from the 3rd and 4th grades will perform.
7:30 P.M. Students from the 5th and 6th grades will perform.
8:00 P.M. Teachers and other staff will perform.
8:30 P.M. The school's drama team will perform.
9:00 P.M. The winners from each group will be announced.
9:15 P.M. Refreshments will be served.

If you want to be in the show and have not already signed up, it's not too late.
Sign up with Mr. Cooper in the main office by Friday afternoon.

26. What is the best summary of the flyer?

Ⓐ The 3rd and 4th graders are holding a talent show.

Ⓑ The track team needs new uniforms.

Ⓒ The school is having a spring talent show.

Ⓓ The staff will be performing in the show.

27. What is the first thing that will happen during the talent show?

Ⓐ Students in the lowest grades will perform.

Ⓑ The teachers will perform.

Ⓒ Refreshments will be served.

Ⓓ The drama team will do a skit.

28. What is the last thing that will happen at the event?

Ⓐ The 5th and 6th graders will perform.

Ⓑ The awards will be handed out.

Ⓒ Refreshments will be served.

Ⓓ The winners will be announced.

29. What is the best summary of why the talent show is being held?

Ⓐ The school wants to find out if there are any superstars there.

Ⓑ The track team needs new uniforms.

Ⓒ The students are being graded on their performances.

Ⓓ The families like seeing their kids up on stage.

30. What detail shows students they can still enter the contest?

Ⓐ It states that students can enter up until Friday afternoon.

Ⓑ It is posted that registration ended the previous day.

Ⓒ It states that the contest is full and no one else can enter.

Ⓓ Registration will not end until Saturday morning.

GO ON TO THE NEXT PAGE ➡

Posttest

Session 2

from **The Egypt Game**
by Zilpha Keatley Snyder

> Read this story about a strange little shop in California and its peculiar owner from the book *The Egypt Game*.

Chapter 1: The Discovery of Egypt

Not long ago in a large university town in California, on a street called Orchard Avenue, a strange old man ran a dusty, shabby store. Above the dirty show windows a faded peeling sign said:

A-Z

Antiques

Curios

Used Merchandise

Nobody knew for sure what the A-Z meant. Perhaps it referred to the fact that all sorts of strange things—everything from A to Z—were sold in the store. Or perhaps it had something to do with the owner's name. However, no one seemed to know for sure what his name actually was. It was all part of a mysterious uncertainty about even the smallest item of public information about the old man. Nobody seemed certain, for instance, just why he was known as the Professor.

The neighborhood surrounding the Professor's store was made up of inexpensive apartment houses, little family-owned shops, and small, aging homes. The people of the area, many of whom had some connection with the university, could trace their ancestors to every continent, and just about every country in the world.

There were dozens of children in the neighborhood; boys and girls of every size and style and color, some of whom could speak more than one language when they wanted to. But in their schools and on the streets they all seemed to speak the same language and to have a number of things in common. And one of the things they had in common, at that time, was a vague and mysterious fear of the old man called the Professor.

Just what was so dangerous about the Professor was uncertain, like everything else about him, but his appearance undoubtedly had something to do with the rumors. He was tall and bent and his thin beard fraggled up his cheeks like dry moss on gray rocks. His eyes were dark and expressionless, and set so deep under heavy brows that from a distance they looked like dark empty holes. And from a distance was the only way that most children of Orchard Avenue cared to see them. The Professor lived somewhere at the back of his dingy store, and when he came out to stand in the sun in his doorway, smaller children would cross the street if they had to walk by.

1. **"...His thin beard fraggled up his cheeks like dry moss on gray rocks." This is an example of which type of figurative language?**

   Ⓐ Simile

   Ⓑ Metaphor

   Ⓒ Idiom

   Ⓓ Personification

2. **Which best describes the setting of the passage?**

   Ⓐ A university town

   Ⓑ The inside of the Professor's apartment

   Ⓒ A city in Egypt

   Ⓓ An aging home on Orchard Avenue

3. **What do the children in the passage have in common?**

   Ⓐ They all have brown hair.

   Ⓑ They all can trace their ancestors back to the same continent.

   Ⓒ They all are afraid of the Professor.

   Ⓓ They all have had the Professor as their teacher.

4. **Which word from the passage contains a suffix meaning "without"?**

   Ⓐ Undoubtedly

   Ⓑ Expressionless

   Ⓒ Doorway

   Ⓓ Surrounding

GO ON TO THE NEXT PAGE ➡

ISAT Coach, Reading Level D, New Edition

5. **Using context clues, what does <u>shabby</u> mean in the first paragraph?**

    Ⓐ Falling apart or dirty

    Ⓑ Clean and new

    Ⓒ Old

    Ⓓ Strange

6. **This passage is an example of which literary type?**

    Ⓐ Myth

    Ⓑ Legend

    Ⓒ Folk tale

    Ⓓ Story

7. **What is the main idea of this passage?**

    Ⓐ There was a mysterious fear of the old man called the Professor.

    Ⓑ Life in a university town is anything but ordinary.

    Ⓒ University towns have people who come from many different cultures.

    Ⓓ Old shops have many hidden treasures.

8. **Which of the following is an opinion?**

    Ⓐ The Professor had a store on Orchard Avenue.

    Ⓑ Orchard Avenue had the best stores of any other street in the university town.

    Ⓒ The Professor's store sold all sorts of strange things.

    Ⓓ The people of the area had some connection to the university.

9. **What is the correct meaning of the homonym <u>store</u> found in paragraph 2?**

    Ⓐ To gather or provide something with other things

    Ⓑ To hold until a later time

    Ⓒ A place where items are sold

    Ⓓ To enter or save data

10. "His eyes were dark and expressionless, and set so deep under heavy brows that from a distance they looked like dark empty holes." This is an example of which literary device?

Ⓐ Idiom

Ⓑ Metaphor

Ⓒ Simile

Ⓓ Assonance

11. Which is a synonym of <u>ancestor</u> in paragraph 3?

Ⓐ Relative

Ⓑ Friend

Ⓒ Classmate

Ⓓ Shopper

12. What is the author's purpose for writing this passage?

Ⓐ To persuade people to shop in specialty stores

Ⓑ To explain how people get nicknames, such as the Professor

Ⓒ To encourage people to visit Egypt

Ⓓ To introduce the setting and characters of the story

13. Which is an antonym of <u>inexpensive</u>?

Ⓐ Cheap

Ⓑ Shabby

Ⓒ Costly

Ⓓ Faded

GO ON TO THE NEXT PAGE ➡

14. **Why do children cross the street when they see the Professor?**

Ⓐ They are afraid of him and want to avoid him.

Ⓑ The Professor won't let them walk in front of his store.

Ⓒ The Professor gets nervous when around children.

Ⓓ There is no other place to walk.

15. **What does the compound word** <u>doorway</u> **mean?**

Ⓐ Escaping from something

Ⓑ The opening of a building or a room

Ⓒ An object used to hold a door open

Ⓓ A piece of rubber that prevents damage to a wall when a door is opened

16. **What is the suffix in** <u>connection</u>?

Ⓐ Con-

Ⓑ Connect

Ⓒ -ion

Ⓓ -nect

17. **"The owners of the newer stores raised their eyebrows at the Professor's dirty show windows." What is the idiom in this sentence?**

Ⓐ "Raised their eyebrows"

Ⓑ "Dirty show window"

Ⓒ "The owners of the newer stores"

Ⓓ "At the Professor"

18. **Which meaning of the homonym** <u>part</u> **fits best with paragraph 2?**

Ⓐ A division or portion of something

Ⓑ The line in a hairstyle

Ⓒ A role in a play

Ⓓ An important feature or part of something

19. " . . . A vague and mysterious fear of the old man called the Professor." What is the meaning of <u>vague</u>?

Ⓐ Uncertain

Ⓑ Clear

Ⓒ Mysterious

Ⓓ Old

20. "Perhaps it referred to the fact that all <u>sorts</u> of <u>strange</u> things— everything from A to Z—were <u>sold</u> in the <u>store</u>." The underlined words are an example of which literary device?

Ⓐ Simile

Ⓑ Metaphor

Ⓒ Alliteration

Ⓓ Consonance

21. "The Professor was the black sheep of the town." Which best explains this idiom?

Ⓐ The Professor is well liked by those in his community.

Ⓑ The Professor is respected by those in his community.

Ⓒ The Professor does not fit in with the others in his community.

Ⓓ The Professor is accepted by those in his community.

22. Which is an antonym of <u>faded</u>?

Ⓐ Dull

Ⓑ Pale

Ⓒ Light

Ⓓ Bright

GO ON TO THE NEXT PAGE ➡

23. What type of character is the Professor?

Ⓐ Main character

Ⓑ Supporting character

Ⓒ Protagonist

Ⓓ Narrator

24. When does this passage take place?

Ⓐ In the future

Ⓑ At the present

Ⓒ Before modern times

Ⓓ In the year 2000

25. What caused the children to be afraid of the Professor?

Ⓐ His strangeness

Ⓑ His love of practical jokes

Ⓒ Peer pressure

Ⓓ Their bravery

26. Which is the best meaning of torment?

Ⓐ Teasing

Ⓑ Encouragement

Ⓒ Daring

Ⓓ Bravery

27. What is the prefix in discouraging?

Ⓐ Dis-

Ⓑ courage

Ⓒ -ing

Ⓓ rage

28. Which of the following is a compound word?

Ⓐ Children

Ⓑ Everything

Ⓒ Surrounding

Ⓓ Undoubtedly

29. **How does the author show that the Professor is scary?**

    Ⓐ Through his conversations with other characters

    Ⓑ In the description of his appearance

    Ⓒ Through the his actions

    Ⓓ In the Professor's own words

30. **What can you infer about the Professor?**

    Ⓐ He is a young man.

    Ⓑ He is a criminal.

    Ⓒ He is a teacher at the university.

    Ⓓ He is an older man.

31. **Explain the idiom "You can't judge a book by its cover." How might this relate to the Professor? Use information from the passage and your own ideas to support your answer.**

GO ON TO THE NEXT PAGE ➡

Session 3

"THE REAL PRINCESS" adapted from
"THE PRINCESS AND THE PEA"

by Hans Christian Anderson

> This passage is famous around the world. It is about a princess and a pea.

There was once a prince, and he wanted to marry a princess, but then she must be a real princess. He traveled right round the world to find one, but there was always something wrong. There were plenty of princesses, but whether they were real he had a hard time discovering; there was always something that was not right about them. So at last he had to come home again, and he was very sad because he wanted a real princess so badly.

One evening there was a terrible storm. The rain poured down in sheets.

In the middle of the storm somebody knocked at the town gate, and the Old King himself went to open it.

It was a princess who stood outside, but she was in a terrible state from the rain and the storm. The water streamed out of her hair and her clothes, it ran in at the top of her shoes and out at the heel, but she said that she was a real princess.

"Well, we shall soon see if that is true," thought the old Queen, but she said nothing. She went into the bedroom, took all the bedclothes off and laid a pea on the bedstead; then she took twenty mattresses and piled them on the top of the pea, and then twenty feather beds on the top of the mattresses. This was where the princess was to sleep that night. In the morning they asked her how she had slept.

"Oh, so badly!" said the princess. "I have hardly closed my eyes the whole night! Heaven knows what was in the bed. I seemed to be lying upon some hard thing, and my whole body is black and blue this morning. It is terrible!"

They saw at once that she must be a real princess. She had felt the pea through twenty mattresses and twenty feather beds. Nobody but a true princess could have such delicate skin.

So the prince took her to be his wife, for now he was sure that he had found a real princess, and the pea was put into the Museum, where it may still be seen if no one has stolen it.

1. **What inference can you make from this story?**

    Ⓐ The pea has been stolen from the museum.

    Ⓑ The prince is quite picky about women.

    Ⓒ Princesses always get caught in the rain.

    Ⓓ The old King does not like the princess.

2. **What kind of story is this?**

    Ⓐ Legend

    Ⓑ Nonfiction

    Ⓒ Folk tale

    Ⓓ Poem

3. **Which word from the passage has a suffix?**

    Ⓐ Bedclothes

    Ⓑ Fearful

    Ⓒ Princess

    Ⓓ Terrible

4. **Which word from the passage is a compound word?**

    Ⓐ Bedroom

    Ⓑ Knocked

    Ⓒ Difficulty

    Ⓓ Museum

GO ON TO THE NEXT PAGE ➡

5. **Which event happens first in this story?**

Ⓐ The princess shows up at the castle in the rain.

Ⓑ The prince is looking for a princess to marry.

Ⓒ There is a terrible storm with thunder and lightning.

Ⓓ The old Queen prepares a bed for the princess.

6. **What do you think the author's purpose was in writing this story?**

Ⓐ To entertain

Ⓑ To teach

Ⓒ To persuade

Ⓓ To inform

7. **What is a synonym of <u>terrible</u>?**

Ⓐ Wonderful

Ⓑ Imaginary

Ⓒ Horrible

Ⓓ Lovely

8. **What is an antonym of <u>delicate</u>?**

Ⓐ Tough

Ⓑ Fragile

Ⓒ Clear

Ⓓ Soft

9. **Which word from the story is a homonym?**

Ⓐ Open

Ⓑ Quite

Ⓒ Right

Ⓓ Twenty

10. **What kind of story usually features gods or goddesses?**

Ⓐ Nonfiction

Ⓑ Poems

Ⓒ Folk tales

Ⓓ Myths

11. **What event in the story shows the climax?**

    Ⓐ The princess arrives in the rain.

    Ⓑ The old Queen makes the bed.

    Ⓒ The pea is put in the museum.

    Ⓓ The princess reports she slept badly.

12. **What event is the resolution of the story?**

    Ⓐ The King lets the princess into the castle.

    Ⓑ The Prince marries the princess.

    Ⓒ The pea is stolen from the museum.

    Ⓓ A terrible storm starts.

13. **Which statement is the best summary of this story?**

    Ⓐ Princes can only marry real princesses.

    Ⓑ A queen makes sure that a princess is real.

    Ⓒ Sleeping on a pea is uncomfortable.

    Ⓓ A museum puts a special pea on display.

14. **What is the word root of discovering?**

    Ⓐ Dis

    Ⓑ Cover

    Ⓒ Discover

    Ⓓ Ing

15. **What implicit main idea is in this passage?**

    Ⓐ It storms often in this kingdom.

    Ⓑ Most castles have peas in the kitchen.

    Ⓒ Princes must marry carefully.

    Ⓓ Kingdoms always have museums.

16. **What is the prefix in <u>discovering</u>?**

Ⓐ Dis-

Ⓑ Cover

Ⓒ -ing

Ⓓ Disco-

17. **What does the compound word <u>bedclothes</u> mean?**

Ⓐ The frame of a bed

Ⓑ Sheets and blankets

Ⓒ Pajamas

Ⓓ Pillows and mattresses

18. **What does the homonym <u>closed</u> mean in paragraph 6?**

Ⓐ Knowing someone very well

Ⓑ Near in space or time

Ⓒ To stop working, or shut down a store or business

Ⓓ To come together or bring the edges of something together

19. **Why did the old Queen stack twenty mattresses on a bed for the princess?**

Ⓐ To make the girl's bed more comfortable

Ⓑ To show the girl how rich the king and queen were

Ⓒ The girl asked to sleep on twenty mattresses

Ⓓ To hide the pea as a test to see if the girl were a real princess

20. **Which shows the correct sequence of events?**

Ⓐ The old Queen places a pea under twenty mattresses, the prince marries the girl, the old King answers the door

Ⓑ The old King answers the door, the prince marries the girl, the old Queen places the pea under the mattresses

Ⓒ The girl arrives at the palace, the old King opens the door, the old Queen places a pea under the mattresses

Ⓓ The old King answers the door, the prince searches for a real princess, the prince marries the girl